Kampuchea: Decade of the Genocide

Edited by Kimmo Kiljunen

Kampuchea: Decade of the Genocide

Report of a Finnish Inquiry Commission

Edited by Kimmo Kiljunen

Zed

Kampuchea: Decade of the Genocide was first published by Zed Books Ltd., 57 Caledonian Road, London N1 9BU, in 1984.

Typeset by Forest Photosetting
Proofread by A.M. Berrett
Cover design by Jacque Solomons
Printed in the UK at The Bath Press, Avon.

1st reprint, 1986.

British Library Cataloguing in Publication Data

Kampuchea.
1. Kampuchea–History–1953–1975
2. Kampuchea–History–Civil War, 1970–1975
3. Kampuchea–History–1975–
I. Kiljunen, Kimmo
959.6'04 DS554.8

ISBN 0-86232-208-1
ISBN 0-86232-209-X Pbk

US Distributor
Biblio Distribution Center, 81 Adams Drive, Totowa, New Jersey 07512

Contents

Maps

Tables

PROVINCES OF KAMPUCHEA

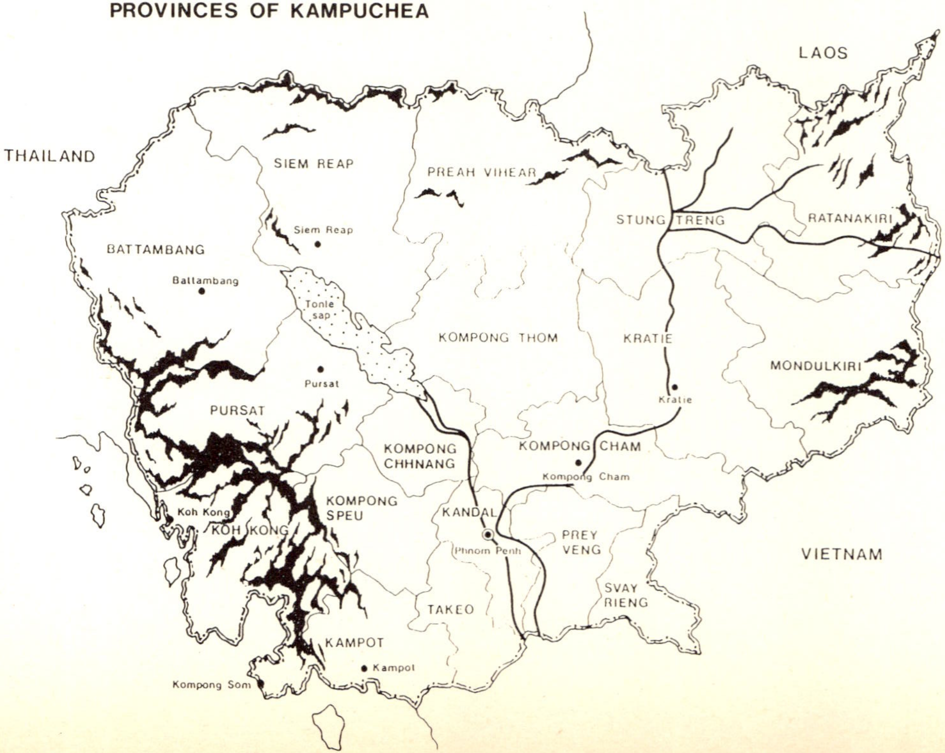

Preface

This book is a revised and re-edited version of the report of the Finnish Inquiry Commission *Kampuchea in the Seventies* published in Helsinki in December 1982.

The Kampuchea Inquiry Commission was established in Helsinki in October 1980 to study the political, social and economic development of Kampuchea and the subsequent legal implications and repercussions on international politics, especially in light of the events of the 1970s. The Commission worked as an autonomous research body independent of any organization or institution.

At the end of the 1960s Kampuchea was a relatively stable and peaceful country, despite the extensive war in neighbouring Vietnam. During the 1970s, however, the people of Kampuchea met with a series of tragedies, the causes and extent of which the Commission wished to examine. The largest estimates of the number of people who died in Kampuchea during that decade have risen to three million, which is equivalent to one third of the entire population. According to international statistics, Kampuchea was the poorest nation in the world at the end of the 1970s.

A number of reasons for this state of affairs have been put forth: the extension of US hostilities into Kampuchea, including widespread bombing at the beginning of the 1970s; the *coup d'état* against Prince Sihanouk and the consequent drawn-out civil war; the repressive politicies of the Pol Pot regime and its massive transfers of population; Vietnam's intervention in the country; starvation and the flood of refugees; and continued military operations along the border with Thailand. An objective examination of the Kampuchean situation has constantly been hampered by the strong connection of great power conflicts with the question.

The purpose of the Kampuchea Inquiry Commission was to study as objectively as possible what really happened in Kampuchea during the 1970s. The study focused on the parties to the civil war in Kampuchea as well as on the role of Vietnam and other neighbouring countries, and the policies of the great powers. Similarly, the reaction of the international community in both relief activities and in the mass media was a subject for examination as was the separate question of Finland's attitude towards the events in Indochina.

When establishing the Inquiry Commission the stand was taken that its purpose could be fulfilled only by adhering to a position of strict neutrality, with no preconceived goal or ambition, nor was the intent to place a blame *a priori* on any party or parties. The purpose was to examine, with a view to better understanding of future international crises, the historical, great power political, regional, social and ideological factors that combined to bring about the catastrophe. Stress was laid on the aspect of human rights in the examination of the events.

The Chairman of the Commission was Professor Helge Gyllenberg of the University of Helsinki; the Secretary-General was Kimmo Kiljunen, Research Fellow at the Academy of Finland. The other members of the Commission were:

Esko Antola	Docent at the University of Turku
Osmo Apunen	Professor at the University of Tampere
Göran von Bonsdorff	Professor at the University of Helsinki
Johan von Bonsdorff	Editor-in-chief of *Ny Tid*
Vilho Harle	Docent at the University of Tampere
Pentti Holappa	Author
Jan-Magnus Jansson	Editor-in-chief of *Huvudstadsbladet*
Ville Komsi	MP
Pekka Kuusi	Former Director-General of Alko
Timo Laatunen	Managing Director of Aamulehti
K.J. Lang	Director-General of the Prison Administration
Paavo Nikula	Counsellor at the Legislative Department of the Ministry of Justice
Allan Rosas	Professor at Abo Akademi
Ensio Siilasvuo	Lt.-Gen. (retd.)
Folke Sundman	Organization Secretary of the UN Association
Helena Tuomi	Research Fellow at the Tampere Peace Research Institute
Erkki Tuomioja	Deputy Mayor of Helsinki
MikkoValtasaari	Head of Section at the Finnish Broadcasting Co.
John Vikström	Archbishop
Reijo Vilenius	Professor at the University of Jyväskylä
Raimo Väyrynen	Professor at the University of Helsinki

The Commission was assisted by five separate research groups at the Universities of Helsinki, Tampere and Turku and at Abo Akademi. The first of these groups, led by Secretary-General Kimmo Kiljunen, has dealt with Kampuchea's historical, political and social development. The other members of the groups were Johan von Bonsdorff, Ari Huhtala and Hannu Reime ja Folke Sundman; the second group was led by Helena Tuomi and investigated the significance of international humanitarian aid in easing the Kampuchean refugee problem and famine. The other members were Gunilla Gustafs, Mervi Gustafsson, Aki Hietanen, Pekka Hiltunen, Juha Holma and Aija Löksy and Helena Rytövuori; the third group was led by Mikko Valtasaari and surveyed coverage of the Kampuchean situation in the information media of various countries and groupings of countries. The other members were Leif Granholm, Jyrki Koulumies, Hannu Reime and Raija Valta; the fourth group was led by Allan Rosas and Esko Antola and it examined the Kampuchean situation as a question of international politics and international law. The other members of this group were Ann-Christine Eriksson, Olli Korhonen, Heli Pelkonen and Anne-Maj Takala; the fifth group was led by Osmo Apunen and it examined Finland's policy towards Indo-China. The other members of the group were Sirpa Kaare, Tarja Seppä and Unto Vesa.

The level of scientific accomplishment required by the grant from the Finnish Academy was overseen by Professor Göran von Bonsdorff; Professor Tapani Valkonen provided expert assistance in the section dealing with population; the maps were drawn by Aila Ulmanen; Katrina Aaltonen assisted in the Commission's technical work; the translation into English is by Eddy Hawkins.

A delegation of the Commission carried out a trip to Kampuchea, Vietnam and Thailand from 15 February to 16 March 1982. The delegation was led by Professor Helge Gyllenberg and included Kimmo Kiljunen and Hannu Reime. During the trip the delegation met over one hundred representatives of the various states, international organizations, international relief groups, political movements and civic organizations spanning the spectrum of the parties to the Kampuchean conflict. Among these were: Foreign Minister of the People's Republic of Kampuchea, Hun Sen; Vietnam's Foreign Minister, Ngyen Co Thach; the Secretary General of Thailand's National Security Council, Gen. Prasong Soonsiri; US Ambassador to Thailand, John G. Dean; Minister-Counsellor of the Soviet Embassy in Kampuchea, Iosif E. Kolesnikov; a representative of Democratic Kampuchea, Bun Kim; the Commander of Prince Sihanouk's Moulinaka movement, Nhem Sophon; and the Commander of the KPNLF front, Gen. Dien Del. In Kampuchea, the delegation visited Phnom Penh and surrounding provinces, as well as Pursat, Battambang, Sisophon and Siem Reap. In Vietnam, visits were made to Saigon and Hanoi as well as to Thay Ninh along the border with Kampuchea and to Lang Son along the border with China. In Thailand, the delegation visited Bangkok and refugee camps in the Kampuchean border area as well as inland.

Chapters 1 to 5 of this book are by the study group led by Kimmo Kiljunen; chapter 7 is by the study group led by Allan Rosas, and chapter 8 by Mikko Vattasaari's group. Chapter 6, by Helena Tuomi's study group is a new addition for this revised version. The final chapter of the original report, dealing with Finnish policy towards Indo-China, and written by Osmo Apunen's group, is omitted here as its relevance was specifically to Finland.

The Commission received support from Finland's Ministry of Education, the Academy of Finland, the Development Co-operation Section of Finland's Ministry for Foreign Affairs, the Nordic Institute for Asian Affairs and the Nordic Co-operation Committee for International Politics.

The Finnish Association for Peace Research acted as the financial bookkepping organization required by provisions concerning the receipt of state aid.

Kimmo Kiljunen
Helsinki

1. Historical Background

by study group led by Kimmo Kiljunen

Up until 1970, Kampuchea was referred to as the Kingdom of Cambodia – a name retained from the period of French colonialism. The sharp social changes of the 1970s, however, have also been seen in changes in the name of the country. After the overthrow of the royal house in 1970, the country was officially referred to as the Khmer Republic. During 1975-8 the country was Democratic Kampuchea and since 1979 it has been the People's Republic of Kampuchea. The violent changes in government which have followed one after the other have stressed the significance of social changes with repeated revisions of national symbols up to and including the national flag and the name of the country. In this report systematic use is made of the name Kampuchea, including when the subject matter concerns periods during which the official form of the country's name was different. However, in passages referring to specific regimes the official name of the period or government may appear.

Kampuchea is located in Indochina; the term Indochina is not only a geographical definition, but also refers to the region's historical past. It lies both geographically and historically in the area between the two ancient cultures of China and India. Throughout history, the region of Indochina has received numerous enriching influences from both directions, but it has also been the object of difficult opposing pressures and contradictions. The northernmost parts of the region, Vietnam and Laos, have traditionally been shaped as a part of the Chinese cultural sphere. On the other hand, the most southerly areas of Indochina, including present-day Kampuchea, have, in terms of cultural heritage, been primarily Indian.

Kampuchea's problems today are centrally tied to the development of the whole of the region of Indochina and its position in the international order. Indochina is, for its part, a section of South-east Asia, a very important area in global great power politics. With the exception of the Indian subcontinent, there is hardly any other part of the world in which the direct security interests and spheres of influence of the three great powers, the United States, the Soviet Union and China, are in the same manner so fundamentally in opposition to one another. Thus, the conflicts caused by sharp internal social contradictions or ethnic and territorial disputes in South-east Asia, when connected with the state of confrontation in international power politics, form a threat to world peace.

The historical development of Kampuchea as a part of the international order during the past two centuries can be divided into six phases:

1. Pre-colonial period.
2. French colonial period (1864-1954) and first Indo-China war (1946- 54);
3. Kingdom of Cambodia (1954-70);
4. Khmer Republic (1970-5) and second Indo-China war (1960-75);
5. Democratic Kampuchea (1975-8);
6. People's Republic of Kampuchea (1979-) and third Indo-China war (1978-).

These various phases in the development of Kampuchean society differ from one another in their internal administration, power relationships and even social systems, as well as in external dependence. The most sudden and the deepest social changes took place during the 1970s at the cost of great human suffering.

The Period of Colonial and Royal Rule

When the French reduced Kampuchea to the status of a protectorate in 1864, they took control of a divided kingdom which had been split into vassel states by neighbouring Vietnam and Thailand. By then, the great age of Kampuchea, when the Khmer Empire from its centre at Angkor Thom had ruled not only modern Kampuchea but also Laos, the southern part of Vietnam, Thailand and parts of Burma as far as to the Gulf of Bengal, was a dim memory. The period of power of the Angkor Dynasty lasted from the 9th to the 15th Centuries. The remains of this military might and the advanced stage of economic and cultural development can still be seen in the great ruins of the temples and palaces of Angkor. The Empire fell apart because of internal power struggles and with the encroachment of the Siamese and Vietnamese its territory gradually came under their control.[1]

The French made Kampuchea part of the Indo-Chinese Federation, which was divided into four protectorates: Annam, Tonkin, Laos and Kampuchea as well as the colony of Cochin China in south Vietnam. Thus, a united political and administrative entity was created in Indo-China, headed by a French governor-general. Under the French colonial system, Kampuchea became a peripheral area into which a great deal of development resources were not expended, rather, the traditional society remained to a large extent intact. The local royal house retained a relative degree of independence. It was not until the 1920s that a systematic effort was begun to exploit the country's natural resources by establishing plantations to produce rubber for export. Trade and enterprise were mainly in the hands of Vietnamese and Chinese, and especially Vietnamese were recruited by the colonial administration to fill the lower positions in the civil service and the police force. This had a part in giving rise to ethnic tensions within the country.

During the Second World War, Japan occupied Kampuchea and declared it independent. Norodom Sihanouk, who had been chosen as king in 1941 at the age of 19, was persuaded by the Japanese to renounce the agreements between Kampuchea and France. The right-wing nationalist Son Ngoc Thanh was named prime minister. After the War, however, France was able for a time to reinstate its colonial administration. During the War, in 1942, a politically and organizationally unco-ordinated movement, the Khmer Issarak, was founded and gradually developed into the umbrella grouping for anti-French guerrilla activities. To a growing extent it co-operated with the Vietnamese liberation movement, the Vietminh. Armed resistance against the French had spread throughout the whole of Indo-China and gradually radicalized the Kampucheans as well. Finally, in 1953, in an attempt to prevent the left from coming to power, France acceded to the demands for independence from the royal house of Kampuchea led by Prince Sihanouk.[2]

The 1954 Geneva Conference brought to an end the first Indo-China war and confirmed Kampuchea's independence and international status. Under the terms of the peace agreement, all foreign troops were to be withdrawn from the country, i.e. all French and Vietnamese units. At the same time it was agreed that no foreign bases were to be established in the country which thus ensured Kampuchea's neutral status. In accordance with the Geneva treaty, an international supervisory commission arrived in the country and stayed there until the end of 1969. The Vietnamese alone represented the leftist guerrilla movements of Indo-China in Geneva – which meant that the Kampuchean political left had no say of its own in the country's plan for independence. Thus, for Sihanouk, the result of the Geneva Conference was very successful in that it strengthened his position in the country's leadership.

In 1955 Prince Sihanouk abdicated in favour of his father in order to retain his position as the head of the executive power. For support he founded a broadly based national movement, the Sankum, which came to dominate the activities of the legislature. In practice Kampuchea became a one party state. The open opposition groups fell apart and their possibilities to carry on activities were suppressed. On the other hand, left and right factions were formed within the Sangkum. The power struggle between these two factions characterized the political development of Kampuchea until the rightist military coup led by Prime Minister Lon Nol in 1970.

The compromise solution reached at the Geneva Conference had defined Kampuchea's international political status as one of neutrality. This supported well Prince Sihanouk's internal political power aims and matched the geopolitical realities of the Indo-Chinese region at that time – the fact was that the background to the first Indo-China war included not only a national liberation struggle, but also an important great power policy dimension. In the last phase of the war the United States had become a major party to the conflict, in the end financing 80% of the cost of France's colonial war.

Following the Chinese Revolution, the Korean War and the defeat suffered by France in Indo-China, an attempt was made by the West to secure a military presence in South-east Asia with the founding of SEATO (South-East Asia Treaty Organization). It formed one link in the chain of military alliances surrounding the Soviet Union during the years of the cold war, and additionally it was aimed against the region's internal leftist revolutionary movements in the name of the 'defence of the free world'. In addition to the United States, the founding members of the alliance were Great Britain, France, Thailand, the Philippines, Pakistan, Australia and New Zealand. It was conceived as also encompassing Kampuchea, Laos and South Vietnam. Kampuchea, however, led by Prince Sihanouk, stressed its neutral status and declined membership of SEATO. On the other hand, Prince Sihanouk was prepared to turn to the United States not only for development aid, but also for acquiring arms aid.

In order to maintain a balance, Sihanouk also established diplomatic relations with China and the Soviet Union and signed agreements on co-operation in trade and economics with both countries. In the United States this kind of *rapprochement* with socialist countries was not looked upon favourably. It began giving covert support to rightist Khmer Serei guerrillas opposed to Sihanouk, which had started guerrilla activities out of South Vietnam and Thailand during the 1950s. Kampuchea's relations cooled with its neighbours, which were dependent on the United States, leading to border clashes. In 1961 Kampuchea broke off diplomatic relations with Thailand, a few years later it ended its military aid programme with the United States, and in the end broke off diplomatic relations with Washington in 1965.

The cessation of American aid had serious economic consequences. Nearly a third of Kampuchea's police force and army had been financed with US support. The external balance of the country's national economy had been built upon economic aid as had the standard of living of the local elite. Thus, the stoppage of American aid forced a change in the direction of economic policy. Politicians promoting a more self-deterministic model of economic development and leftist views who had been named to the government, such as Khieu Samphan, Hou Youn and Hu Nim, gained a foothold in Sihanouk's administration. Under the leadership of then Minister of the Economy, Khieu Samphan, private banks and financial institutions were nationalized while foreign trade was brought under public control.

The new economic policy and the freezing of relations with the United States, however, caused a reaction in those strata of the population – the army officer corps, the upper levels of the civil service, import-export traders, large landholders – who felt their earlier privileges threatened and who to a large extent still held the reins of social power. At the same time Kampuchea's external environment changed as the Americans became ever more actively involved in Vietnam's internal development. By the mid-1960s there were already a half a million American troops in Vietnam and individual clashes had escalated into a large-scale war. For Vietnam's resistance movement, Kampuchea's neutral status was ideal. Being outside the war it provided a sheltered environment for the FNL's logistics connections. Very soon, however, the Americans extended their military operations to cover the whole of Indo-China.

The Americans also attempted to give more direct support to rightist forces inside Kampuchea than they had given earlier. Following elections in 1966, the right, under the leadership of Lon Nol and Sirik Matak, gained the upper hand in the country's internal development. The government and the civil service were purged of leftists, a significant number of whom – including Khieu Samphan, Hou You and Hu Nim – fled to the countryside in 1967 with the aim of organizing armed resistance to the rightist government policy. In 1967 and 1968 there were peasant uprisings in the country. The government took harsh measures to put down these rebel movements, which had the effect of gradually broadening the rebel Khmer Rouge movement.

In 1969 diplomatic relations were re-established with the United States. The terms of American aid were a change to a more open economic policy and a more favourable attitude to foreign investment. The production sectors which had been nationalized and the financial sector were to be returned to private ownership, and the regulation of foreign trade was to be ended. It was also in US interests to make the Kampuchean army a direct participant in the Vietnam War. In this respect Sihanouk's aim of neutrality formed an increasingly difficult barrier to US strategic operations in Indo-China. On 18 March 1970 he was overthrown in a military coup led by Lon Nol: the Kingdom of Cambodia was abolished and the Khmer Republic was established. In April a large-scale military operation by the Americans and South Vietnamese began in south-eastern Kampuchea with the entry of a force of 20,000 men. The Vietnam war had been transformed into an Indo-Chinese war.[3]

The Khmer Republic

One aspect of the background to the overthrow of Sihanouk was the internal political struggle over which alternative for development to follow: a socialist, self-reliant line, or an open line based on market forces. Another aspect was the confrontation between a policy of neutrality and an alignment with the United States. The immediate cause of the overthrow of Sihanouk was the need of the United States to secure the area for the Saigon government while gradually disengaging itself and 'Vietnamizing' the war in Indo-China.[4]

The human and material losses in the Vietnam War in Kampuchea were enormous: an estimated 600,000 people – that is, nearly 10% of the population – died as a result of the war. Massive bombing of the rural areas led to a flood of refugees who crowded into the cities under the control of the Lon Nol government. By the time the war ended in 1975 an estimated over one third of the rural population – some two million people – had become refugees, and this meant a near complete breakdown of the traditional social structure. The population of Phnom Penh alone, within five years rose from some 600,000 to over two million. The population experienced actual famine because of the disruption of agricultural production and the break in connections with the countryside.[5]

Already during the year immediately following the military coup by Lon Nol there was a sharp decline in production of the country's most important food crop, rice, and production of the most important export product, rubber, in practice came to a halt. During the next year, 1972, the rice harvest was less than half of that of the previous year and the situation only worsened as the following Table 1 shows.

Table 1
Agricultural Production 1968-74 (thousands of tonnes)

	1968/69	*1969/70*	*1970/71*	*1971/72*	*1972/73*	*1973/74*
Rice	2,503	3,814	2,732	2,138	953	762
Rubber	51	52	13	1	15	12
Maize	117	137	121	80	73	—
Palm Sugar	—	34	23	—	—	—

Source: Economist Intelligence Unit, *Quarterly Economic Report, Annual Supplement 1975.*

Military actions destroyed crops and disrupted transport connections. After the war it was estimated that 75% of all domestic animals had been destroyed. The survival of the urban population depended almost entirely on deliveries of rice by the Americans. The prices of basic foodstuffs rose dramatically. For example, a kilogram of rice which had cost eight riels in 1970, cost ten times as much in 1974 and its cost rose by a factor of four by February 1975 to 340 riels.[6]

As a result of the war the country's small industrial sector also suffered heavy damage. Of the 1,400 rice mills that had been in operation only 300 were still working in 1974 and only 65 of the previous sawmills were in use. The country's only phosphate plant and only paper mill were completely destroyed. Similarly, cement and textile production facilities suffered serious damage. Of the roads, 40% were entirely unfit for use and one third of the country's bridges had been blown up. For the most part this damage had been caused by US bombing in 1973.

The country's traditional export items were rubber, rice and corn. Even though it was possible to restart rubber production, export earnings did not cover 11% of imports in 1973. The country's balance of trade collapsed irreparably into deficit. The inclusion of the balance of services increases even more the balance of payments deficit as can be seen from Table 2.

Table 2
Foreign Trade (millions of Special Drawing Rights)

	1969	*1970*	*1971*	*1972*	*1973*	*1974*
Exports	65.9	41.2	13.1	6.4	4.9	1.2
Imports	99.2	68.6	55.1	65.5	42.0	22.8
Services (net)	– 1.2	– 2.6	– 11.6	– 24.0	– 8.2	–
Goods and services (net)	– 34.5	– 30.0	– 53.6	– 83.1	45.3	– 21.6 (estimated)

Source: Economist Intelligence Unit, op. cit.

Economic chaos and external dependence complemented the internal weakness, open corruption and abuses of the Lon Nol administration. The economy was based on service activities dependent upon American aid and on the black market. The state's finances did not function. Leading civil servants and the officer corps exploited the machinery of the state as a means to acquire personal wealth. An increasing share of scarce resources went for military expenditures. Already in 1970 military spending exceeded the state's total revenues. By 1973 this gap had more than doubled. The Lon Nol administration remained intact only with the support of aid from the United States.

Corruption was especially rampant in army circles. It was typical that the commanders of military units entered on their pay-lists even entire 'phantom' companies for which they pocketed the salaries received from the Americans; they also sold weapons and supplies on the black market which often ended up in the hands of the opposing side. The fighting morale of the Lon Nol army was low and it was unable to resist the advance by more experienced Vietnamese troops and the growing number of Kampuchean guerrillas. The situation was not improved even by the large degree of fire support supplied by the United States air force, rather the Americans became even more deeply involved militarily in the war in Kampuchea.[7]

From Peking, following his overthrow, Prince Sihanouk urged the Kampucheans to rise in opposition to the military government. His appeal had an effect especially on the peasantry, which had a traditionally strong loyalty to the royal house and which was alienated from the urban upper class, leading civil servants, officers, large traders and intelligentsia upon whose support the Lon Nol administration had originally been built. The National United Front of Kampuchea, FUNK, was founded: it included not only Sihanouk's supporters, but also local communists who had previously opposed Sihanouk, so-called Khmer Rouge, and leftists who had fled to Vietnam during the 1950s.

It was the Khmer Rouge, which had been a small isolated group of a few thousand members at the beginning of the 1970s, which succeeded in gaining operative control of the resistance movement by 1973. The guerrilla army, radicalized by the brutal war and massive bombings, rapidly grew into a force of 70,000, and the communists with their higher degree of internal organization, discipline and thus efficiency took charge of its leadership.[8]

The Khmer Rouge rejected all opportunities for compromise and began implementing ever more authoritarian administrative methods to ensure their own success, and also the livelihood of the population in the badly damaged rural areas. New soldiers were typically recruited from the poorest population strata of the villages, often from among those who had been orphaned or left homeless. The recruits were young and uneducated, but extremely disciplined and loyal to their leaders. When given command they were stamped by their intolerance and unreasonableness.

The wide-scale bombings had undoubtedly also strengthened the hardest and most reckless elements in the resistance movement. Having visited the liberated areas of Kampuchea in 1973, Prince Sihanouk, who had been reduced to the role of merely representing Kampuchea internationally, asked Chou En Lai to warn Kissinger that the longer the war continued the more radical its outcome would be. Only the withdrawal of American support for the Phnom Penh government could end the war.

Kampuchea under Prince Sihanouk in the 1960s had made an effort to remain isolated from the Vietnam war. Sihanouk, however, had to permit FNL logistic connections to go through his country and had thus attempted to keep Kampuchea's territory outside the scope of actual military operations. Sihanouk was also prepared to recognize the legitimacy of the goals of the nationalist movements in neighbouring countries, despite the fact they may have diverged sharply in social ideology from the path of development chosen by royal Kampuchea. In fact by maintaining good relations with the leftist governments and nationalist movements in neighbouring countries, Sihanouk was able to ensure for himself the freedom of movement needed to suppress activities by domestic leftists within Kampuchea.

For its part, the United States was aiming at a global containment of the 'communist threat' which meant a suppression of the nationalist movement led by Vietnam's communists. In the end, this attempt meant the loss of Kampuchea's national self-determination and the overthrow of the anti-communist government.

Notes

1. About the history of Kampuchea see for example John Audric, *Angkor and the Khmer Empire*, Robert Hale Co., Great Britain, 1972; C.P. Fitzgerald, *A Concise History of East Asia*, Pelican Books, Harmondsworth, 1978; Martin F. Herz, *A Short History of Cambodia*, Frederick A. Praeger Inc., New York, 1958; M.L. Manih Jumsai, *History of Thailand and Cambodia*, Chalermint, Bangkok, 1970.

2. About French colonial rule see for example Milton E. Osborne, *The French Presence in Cochinchina and Cambodia, Rule and Response (1859-1905)*, Cornell University Press, Ithaca, 1969; Roger M. Smith, 'The Khmer Empire, French Rule and the Path to Independence' in J.S. Grant, L.A.G. Moss and J. Unger (eds.), *Cambodia, The Widening War in Indo-China*, Washington Square Press, New York, 1971; J. Davidson, *Indo-China: Signposts in the Storm*, Longman Malaysia, 1979.
3. See Malcolm Caldwell and Lek Tan, *Cambodia in the Southeast Asian War*, Monthly Review Press, New York, 1973; Milton Osborne, *Before Kampuchea: Preludes to Tragedy*, George Allen & Unwin, London, 1979; Roger M. Smith, *Cambodia's Foreign Policy*, Cornell University Press, 1965; Wilfred Burchett, *The Second Indochina War*, International Publishers, New York, 1970; Norodom Sihanouk, *My War with the CIA*, Penguin Books, 1973; Noam Chomsky, *At War with Asia*, Vintage, 1970; Gabriel Kolko, *The Roots of American Foreign Policy*, Beacon Press, Boston, 1969; Serge Thion, 'Dans les Maquis cambodgiens', *Le Monde*, 26-28 April 1972.
4. Leon Boramy and Malcolm Caldwell, 'Behind the Cambodian Coup', *The Spokesman*, No.5, Summer 1970; Michael Leifer, 'Rebellion or Subversion in Cambodia', *Current History*, February 1969.
5. William Shawcross, *Sideshow: Kissinger, Nixon and the Destruction of Cambodia*, Fontana Paperbacks, 1980; Malcolm Caldwell and Lek Tan, op. cit.; and Jonathan Grant et. al., *Cambodia: The Widening War in Indochina*, Washington Square Press, 1971.
6. Economist Intelligence Unit, *Quarterly Economic Report, Annual Supplement, 1975*.
7. See for example Sheldon W. Simon, 'The Role of Outsiders in the Cambodian Conflict', *Orbis* 1/1975 and Noam Chomsky and Edward S. Herman, *After the Cataclysm*, Nottingham, 1979.
8. Michael Vickery, 'Looking Back at Cambodia', *Westerly*, December 1976; Noam Chomsky, *For Reason of State*, Vintage, 1973; Stephen Heder, 'Kampuchea, Armed Struggle, The Origins of an Independent Revolution', *Bulletin of Concerned Asian Scholars*, Vol.11, No.1, 1979.

2. Democratic Kampuchea

When the Lon Nol government surrendered on 17 April 1975 to the peasant army which had surrounded Phnom Penh, the victors won control of a country in a state of chaos. Refugees had increased the size of the capital's population many times over. With the end of American deliveries of rice, famine threatened. Epidemics spread through the slums of the city and the hospitals were unable to treat the wounded. The roads had been destroyed by bombings and in practice industries no longer existed. Any government whatsoever in a similar situation would have been forced to make painful cuts to stave off famine and to get reconstruction under way. The urban population, which had increased dramatically during the war, was simply transferred immediately and entirely to the countryside. The cities were emptied within a few days and the people were forced to plant rice, dig canals and perform other agricultural tasks on collective farms. As the same time, thousands of leading civil servants and officers of the losing side were executed.[1]

The decision to evacuate the cities could not have been based primarily on concern for ensuring the livelihood of the population in a war-ravaged country because the sudden and violent emptying of the cities was carried out at such a high human cost. One explanation has been that the ideological support of the Khmer Rouge was drawn from the interests of the poorest of the peasantry. In primitive agrarian communism the destruction of the classes was to take place on the conditions of the rural poor so that the class position and way of life of the other population groups would fall to the level of the poorest peasantry. These ideological bases for the decision to empty the cities are indicated by the orderliness and throughness of the evacuation, and by the fact that already during the civil war in 1973, when a start was made at collectivizing agriculture, the cities then under the control of the Khmer Rouge were emptied.[2]

Guerrilla soldiers were recruited mainly from among the rural poor, and the level of ideological and political education of the troops was very low. A primitive reaction was the repulsion felt towards the cities and their parasitic inhabitants who had maintained oppression. Furthermore, the peasants and their families who had fled to the cities from the areas of fighting during the war were considered deserters or even traitors. These factors played a part in leading to the abrupt and violent emptying of the cities.

The most crucial consideration in the decision to evacuate the cities, however, was security. Despite their victory, the organization of the Khmer Rouge at the time of the transfer of power was relatively weak and above all inexperienced in ruling the whole of society. Local forces were poorly armed and their ties with the central leadership were loose. There were still remnants of organized resistance by elements of the previous government in the cities.[3] There was the possibility that the economic crisis could have crumbled the basis of the new administration, that Sihanouk could have organized the opposition and that disorganized groups of refugees could have corrupted the earlier-liberated areas. Only by scattering the whole population throughout the countryside was it possible to gain internal security and ensure absolute control over the population.

In order to intensify control on the one hand and to open new areas for cultivation on the other, a second major transfer of population was carried out at the end of 1975. At that time hundreds of thousands of people transferred from the south and east of Phnom Penh were forced to move into the north-western areas of Kampuchea. The third large transfer of population was carried out in the final year of the Khmer Rouge period in power when an uprising in the eastern parts of the country was put down in an extremely bloody manner. In addition to these, a number of smaller population transfers were implemented (see Maps 1 and 2).

The Khmer Rouge

It is impossible to know how unanimously the Communist Party leadership formulated its most important political solutions, one of which was undoubtedly the evacuation of the urban population. For historical reasons the Party has always been internally very divided. Underground activities and the fighting which began in different parts of the country at different times during the 1960s had made it necessary to leave a lot of the power for decision making with the local cadres. But despite past and expected future difficulties, the central Party leadership, which since the 1960s had been comprised of Pol Pot (formerly known as Saloth Sar), Nuon Chea, Ieng Sary and Son Sen, was able to show in April 1975 that the line it had chosen had been correct. The downfall of Sihanouk in the spring of 1970 had offered the Party a unique tactical opportunity to declare their struggle for 'national liberation' in Sihanouk's name and this fight had now been carried through to a victorious conclusion. 'We began with empty hands', as Pol Pot later put it. Kampuchea's internal social disunity, together with outside pressures, provided a small and well organized group the possiblity to bring a large group of peasants under its influence and in the end to gain control of the whole country as a result of civil war.

POPULATION TRANSFERS APRIL 1975

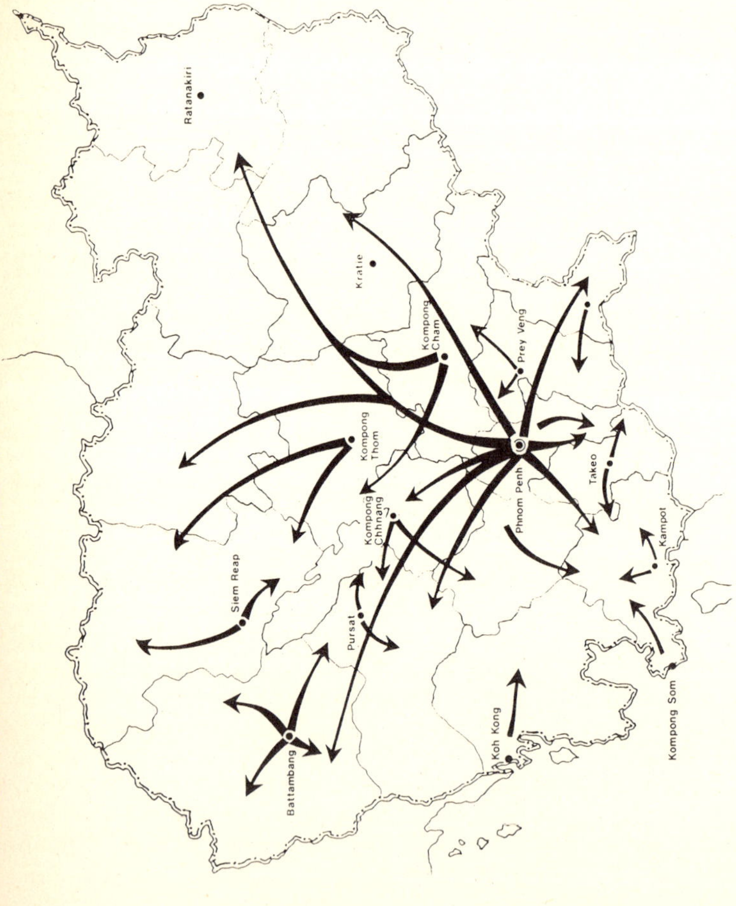

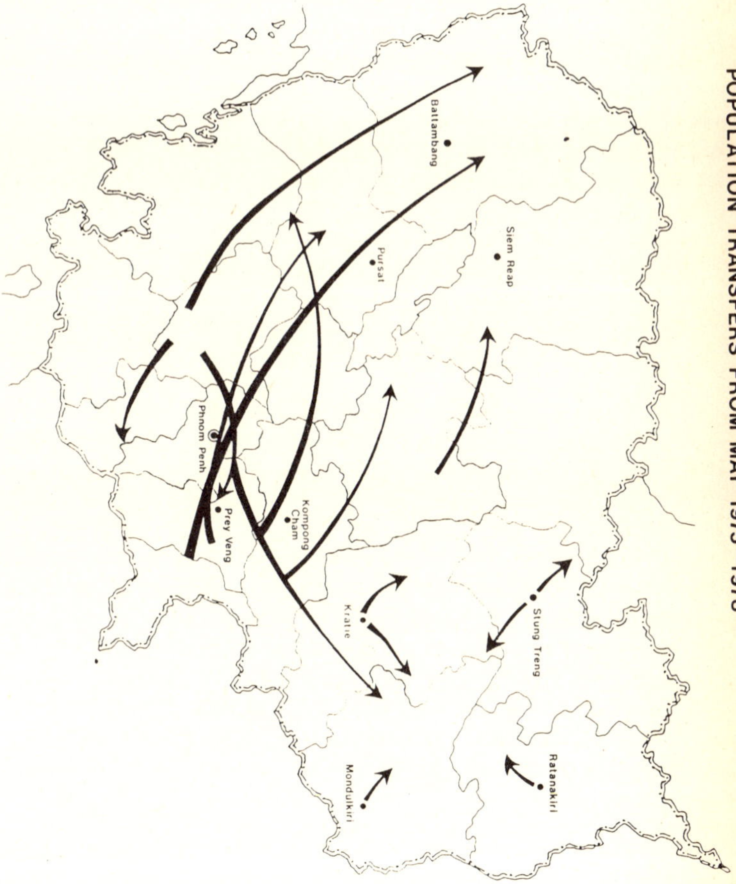

POPULATION TRANSFERS FROM MAY 1975–1978

The secrecy in which the leadership of the Communist Party of Kampuchea had orginally cloaked itself for tactical reasons prevented the outside world from getting sufficient information on the political and social goals of the victors once the war had ended. There were even observers who believed that the country would return to the state of the Sihanouk period, only without its corruption and worst social injustices. The closing of the borders and the complete isolation from the outside world, as well as the immediate evacuation of urban dwellers to the countryside, were a surprise to even the most experienced Kampuchea-watchers.

Those who began ruling Kampuchea in the spring of 1975 were unknown abroad, and once in power they did not pull back very far the curtain of secrecy which obscured them. For a year, the country was still considered a kingdom and Prince Sihanouk regarded as its formal head of state. In fact the ruler, who had returned to his country, was in the Royal Palace under house arrest. The old kingdom became Democratic Kampuchea in the summer of 1976 and Khieu Samphan became its new head of state. References to FUNK decreased and soon ended altogether. The leadership of the country was said to be comprised of an ill-defined revolutionary organization which was called simply the Angkar (organization). The existence of the Communist Party was officially confirmed only in autumn 1977[4]

During the civil war, Khieu Samphan, Hou Youn and Hu Nim were the best known representatives of the Kampuchean left and they were also usually among those mentioned in FUNK propaganda aimed abroad. All three were leftists who had fled from Sihanouk's police out of Phnom Penh to guerrilla bases in the countryside. During the 1950s they had studied in Paris and after returning home had participated in legal institutions created by Sihanouk: the Sangkum Party, the National Assembly; and at the beginning of the 1960s, in Sihanouk's governments. Their connection with the Communist Party and their position in it are unclear. As far as is known they did not, however, belong to the top level of the Party hierarchy. The Party leadership was in the hands of the commanders of the guerrilla army. The Party Secretary Pol Pot, was responsible for the army's military operations. Nuon Chea, who acted as Pol Pot's deputy, was the supreme political commissar of the liberation army. The top military leadership also included Son Sen, who later became the Defence Minister of Democratic Kampuchea. Thus, after the transfer of power in 1975, FUNK political leaders known also abroad did not begin to rule, but rather the real power remained with the military leadership and the seemingly closed, secretive Communist Party which stood behind it.[5]

Living conditions

Living conditions in Democratic Kampuchea differed greatly in both place and time.[6] Local differences sprang from the extensive lack of cohesion in the country's administrative structure and in part form the related policy and personality disagreements within the Party. The most severe repression and the worst wave of executions seems to have taken place during the final phase of Khmer Rouge rule, especially in 1978 when the Party's internal purge reached its widest extent. At the same time the conflict with Vietnam sharpened – this was caused in part by attempts by the Pol Pot faction to reinforce its power. In 1977 especially, Pol Pot calculatedly provoked border clashes by allowing his troops to attack across the border and kill Vietnamese civilians.

Administratively, Democratic Kampuchea was divided into seven zones according to the points of the compass: North, North-east, East, South-west, West, North-west, Cental Zone and the separate zone of Kratie (see map 3). The zones were subdivided into regions, these regions into districts and the districts into villages (co-operatives). The zones and regions of Democratic Kampuchea did not coincide with the provinces of pre-1975 or post-1979 administrations.

In Democratic Kampuchea 95-97% of the population lived on collective farms, of which there were estimated to be well over a thousand. The Kampuchean Communists' collectivization programme was already started in May 1973 during the civil war and at the time that American air bombing was at its most intensive. The purpose of the collective farms was to quickly improve the foodstuffs supply in the warring country and to provide support for the Front and its armed forces in the form of both food and new military recruits.

Gradually, all land, draught animals and means of production were collectivized. At first membership in the co-operative collectives was voluntary, but most people joined to ensure themselves a daily ration of food. By 1974 it became mandatory to join the collectives and some of the dissatisfied peasants fled to the cities under the control of the Lon Nol government. In principle, the results of work on the collectives were divided according to need equally among the families. Part of the production went for the use of the district guerrilla army and part was exchanged through the central organization for various goods such as clothing, motor oil and salt. During the war, the goal was that each collective farm attain the largest possible degree of self-sufficiency. The market mechanism ceased functioning and finally an end was put to the use of money in 1974. The structure of this collective economy created under conditions of war was later used as such as the basic structure of post-war society. The crucial new addition was the reception of the some three million people who were suddenly transferred from the cities to the countryside.

The reception the new people got was unfriendly: they were considered politically suspect, for among other reasons because some of them had moved during the war into enemy controlled cities and had not joined in the struggle in the countryside. On the other hand, the ideological goal of the Communist Party was the creation of a classless society, so an effort was made to destroy the special features of the 'new people' which had been

ADMINISTRATIVE ZONES OF DEMOCRATIC KAMPUCHEA 1975–78

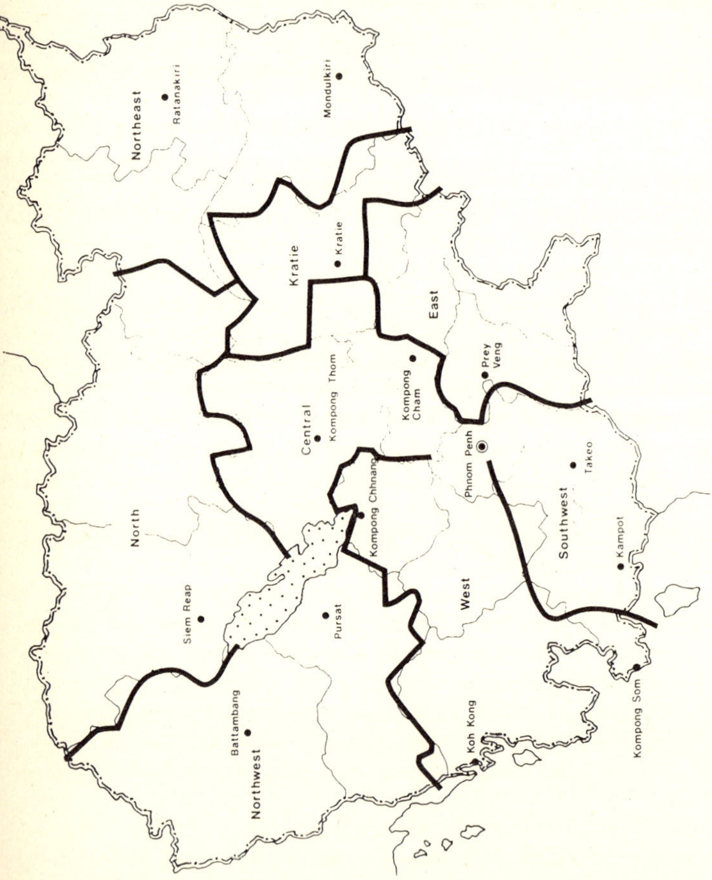

created by the urban economy. This was attempted by reducing them to performing the hardest physical labour in the manner of the poorest of the peasants. The aim was not so much the physical elimination of the representatives of the former intelligentsia and the middle and upper classes as it was the destruction of social structures maintained by these classes.

Members of the intelligentsia were thus not persecuted just because of their formal education even though they were regarded with suspicion, a fact which was demonstrated when thousands of people with this kind of background fled to Thailand after the fall of the Khmer Rouge. According to what was believed up until that time they all should have been dead; many had concealed their former backgrounds. The fact that a significant number of former urban dwellers were the targets of persecution and execution sprang from their understandably disloyal attitude and their readiness to protest against the orders of young, uneducated black-shirted soldiers.

On the collectives, people were divided into various categories in a very hierarchical manner. The basic division was between the 'new' and the 'old' people. The Khmer Rouge system of administration was based on the loyality they enjoyed from the peasants of the areas under their control during the war. With the aim of reinforcing this loyality the urban population – which formerly had been regarded as an élite – was reduced to the most abject conditions on the collective farms. The 'new people' were forced to do the heaviest work; their food and housing were bleak; their families were often broken up; and, for example, they did not receive medicines in the same quantity as the 'old people'. This distinction varied widely from one area to another, and by the end of the Pol Pot period the difference between the living conditions of the 'new' and the 'old' people disappeared almost entirely.

Soldiers, village leaders and the cadres of the Communist Party were recruited from among the poorest of the peasantry: typically they were young, even small teenage boys. The fanaticism and intolerance of the young were thus exploited in building a new society. Supervision of the collective farms was in their hands and often also an absolute power which could lead to random executions for the merest show of insubordination.

Life on the collectives was extremely monotonous and it was attempted to do away with any individuality. The week consisted of ten days and each tenth day was used for 'political education' when mass meetings were held in which discussions mainly concerned improvements in work pratices and increased work efficiency. Long working days were spent in the rice paddies or in digging irrigation canals. Not only was production collectivized, but also consumption, when collective meals were introduced in 1977. Trade by individuals was, in general, not possible – if only for the reason that money was not in use. Thus, neither was there any real system of wages. Through the collective, people received their meagre food rations and a simple black garment. Life outside the collective farms was impossible. On some collective farms men and women were segregated and meetings between married couples were limited. Extramarital sexual relations were forbidden and in some places even forced marriages were arranged.

In addition to the fact that the ending of the use of money and direct physical control bound people to the collectives, the Kampucheans lived a life of isolation from both one another and the outside world. There were no postal or telephone services, or any mass media except for the radio and a newspaper which appeared irregularly and which had a very restricted circulation. Books and libraries were not used; the educational system functioned on a primitive level or not at all; the level of medical services was also very low, often being based on the use of herbs and other folk remedies because imported medicines were banned and hospitals were not functioning. The practice of religion was forbidden and the pagodas were systematically destroyed.

Not only did each of the collective farms attempt to get by on its own as much as possible, but also the whole of the national economy was characterized by a striving for self-reliance and even autarky. In this respect Democratic Kampuchea was isolated from the outside world. Foreign trade was extremely limited: during 1977-8, some rice was exported and was exchanged through trading houses in Hong Kong and Singapore for essential goods. What industry there was in the country used local materials to produce simple consumer goods – clothes, dishes, building materials, tools, for instance.

These facilities were mainly a matter of small workshops. The long-term goal was a sufficiently developed level of industrialization, but one implemented on the basis of local production prerequisites and thus as far as possible independent of imported production elements. There were Chinese and North Korean advisers in the country, but otherwise Kampuchea was completely closed to the outside world. There was only one regular international air connection into the country, a scheduled Chinese flight which flew from Peking to Phnom Penh every other week.

Internal conflicts

The Communist Party was internally fractured, a situation which was reflected in the great deal of power held by regional Party and military leaders. The army units under their control made them to a large degree independent of orders from the Central Committee. Pol Pot and the other members of the Politburo did not themselves have this kind of a personal military support group when, at the end of the war, they moved into Phnom Penh. It was only in July 1975 that the diverse military units were united into a single national army. Following this, the secretaries of the regional Party Committees, Khoy Thuon in the North, Nhim Ros in the North-west, So Phim in the East, Vorn Vet (Sok Thuok) in the special area around Phnom Penh and Ta Mok in the South-west, exercised the real power in their regions where the Central Committee's influence was limited or non-existent.

Internal political activity in Democratic Kampuchea was to a large extent coloured by the power struggle between the Central Committees and the Committees at the zone level. The various regions also differed greatly from one another in terms of living conditions and the extent of repression. The best organized and functioning zones were the South-west and East zones. In the purge which began in the summer of 1975, the Party leadership allied itself with the Party Secretary of the South-west zone. Ta Mok, and his security chief, Duch, in order to gain control of the whole country.

Duch took over the political police, the Nokorbal, which maintained the notorious Tuol Sleng prison in Phnom Penh. It was there that nearly twenty thousand opponents of the Party leadership, or often those only imagined to be opponents, lost their lives after brutal interrogations and forced confessions. Tuol Sleng with its evidence fell intact into the hands of the Vietnamese in January 1979 when the Kampuchean Party leadership fled from Phnom Penh.[7]

Of the regional Party Secretaries, Koy Thuon was purged at the beginning of 1976 and Nhim Ros a year later, So Phim in May 1978 and Vorn Vet in November 1978. So Phim who was also the Deputy Speaker of the Council of State; President Khieu Samphan's first deputy died in the East zone in the spring of 1978 in a rebillon which had broken out against the central government. Living conditions in the East zone had been in general more tolerable, and the policies followed had been less harsh than elsewhere in the country.

The central government attempted to gradually concentrate power, reduce the internal autonomy of the collective farms and cut back on the independence of the regional leadership. This goal was not reached painlessly and the method chosen was a series of widespread purges among the cadres of the collectives. Centralization also had economic consequences: sharp cuts in food rations on the collectives had to be made as ever-larger shares of produce were transferred to the state distribution organization. This led to rebel movements, the most serious threat to Pol Pot's leadership coming from an uprising in the East zone. It was ruthlessly crushed by the action of troops loyal to the central government who were sent in. Tens of thousands of people were killed or transferred to the North and North-west zones, where mass murders of the transferees continued. Some of the rebels were able to flee to Vietnam; they then formed the basis for the Kampuchean National United Front of National Salvation (KNUFNS), which was founded in 1978 and which later, with the support of Vietnamese troops, rose to power in Phnom Penh.

The rebels were accused of being traitors, especially because of their co-operation with Vietnam. It is, however, hardly believable that it would have been possible to find a group within the Party with any real leanings towards the Vietnamese. Those really in sympathy with the Vietnamese, the cadres who had fled to Hanoi in the 1950s and returned to Kampuchea in 1970, had been eliminated during the anti-American civil war. Those individuals such as So Phim were not sympathetic to the Vietnamese, rather their disagreement with the Central Committee was mainly concerned with the tactical question of how to regard Vietnam. As leaders of areas bordering on Vietnam, they opposed the anti-Vietnam policy practised by the central leadership, which can be characterized as chauvinistic, provocative and even racist. This near-mystical chauvinism, which harked back to the glories of the age of the Angkor dynasty, was directed especially against Vietnam. Vietnam was seen as historically expanding its influence and territory at the expense of the Khmers and striving to subjugate Kampuchea. Even since the fall of Democratic Kampuchea, when its leaders admitted to making mistakes, there has remained a desire to place the blame on 'agents of Vietnam' operating in the country, and at the same it has been implied that the mistake was that sufficiently effective action was not taken against these 'agents'.

Democratic Kampuchea came into being under very special and difficult conditions: in comparison with the Vietnamese, it was much harder for the Kampuchean Communists to attain the leadership of the kind of nationalist, independence oriented movement which had sprung up in Indo-China during the Second World War. The Kampucheans did not succeed in this although it was undoubtedly their aim. Only under exceptional conditions – when Kampuchea's social order had fallen apart because of internal contradictions and external pressure – did the Kampuchean Communists gain control of the leadership of the national liberation movement. But then their own conflicts were to affect the whole country.

There are grounds, however, to argue that by the end of 1978 Kampuchea was finding solutions to its various basic material problems such as the food supply, clothing and housing, and at the same time creating the prerequisites for an economic revival. Canals, bridges and dikes were constructed and simple agricultural tools and building materials were produced. Even so, the system collapsed within a few weeks after the arrival of Vietnamese troops and the beginning of the rebellion supported by them. Whatever the material achievements of Democratic Kampuchea it was clear that the nation's psychological condition had been exhausted. Frustration and fatigue had spread also among those peasants who had previously been loyal to the Khmer Rouge administration. Thus attitudes had ripened for a social change to put an end to the existing rule regardless of the nature of the change or the powers behind it.

Notes

1. Ben Kiernan, 'Social Cohesion in Revolutionary Cambodia, *Australian Outlook*, Vol.30, No.3, December 1976; Nayan Chanda, 'When the Killing Had to Stop', *Far Eastern Economic Review*, 29 October 1976 and Karl D. Jackson, 'Cambodia 1978: War, Pillage and Purge in Democratic Kampuchea', *Asian Survey*, Vol.XIX, No.1, 1979.

2. This argument is presented by François Ponchaud, *Cambodia Year Zero*, Penguin Books, 1978.
3. See Frank Snepp, *Decent Interval*, Vintage, 1978. Snepp was in the service of the CIA in Saigon. According to him there were preparations made in Phnom Penh for sabotage against the new government.
4. Pol Pot, 'Les Grandioses Victoires de la Révolution du Kampuchea sous la Direction Juste et Clairvoyante du Parti Communiste du Kampuchea', Ministère des Affaires Etrangeres, Phnom Penh, 1977.
5. *The leaders of the Khmer Resistance and Members of the Royal Government of National Union in the Interior of Cambodia*, NUFC Press, 1972; Timothy Carney, 'Communist Party Power in Kampuchea (Cambodia)', *Documents and Discussions*, Cornell University, 1977; and Serge Thion and Ben Kiernan, *Khmers Rouges! Matériaux pour l'histoire du communisme au Cambodge*, Albin Michel, Paris, 1981.
6. Some of the best presentations about the life and internal development in Democratic Kampuchea are: Ben Kiernan and Chantou Boua, *Peasants and Politics in Kampuchea 1942-81*, Zed Press, London, 1982; Serge Thion and Ben Kiernan, op.cit.; Stephen Heder, 'Kampuchea: From Pol Pot to Pen Sovan to the Villages' in Khien Theeravit and MacAllister Brown (eds.), *Indochina and the Problems of Security and Stability in Southeast Asia,* Chulalongkorn University Press, Bangkok, 1981; Laura Summers, 'Democratic Kampuchea', in Bogdan Szajkowski (ed.), *Marxist Governments: A World Survey*, Macmillan, London, 1979; Laura Summers, 'Co-operatives in Democratic Kampuchea', mimeo, 1981; Michael Vickery, *Cambodia 1975-1980*, South End Press, Boston; Govena McGormack, 'The Kampuchean Revolution 1975-78: The Problem of Knowing the Truth', *Journal of Contemporary Asia*, No.1/2, 1980; Justus M. van der Kroef, 'Political Ideology in Democratic Kampuchea', *Orbis*, Vol.22, 4, 1978-9. See also Jan Myrdal, *Democratic Kampuchea*, Autumn 1979 and George Hildebrand and Gareth Porter, 'Cambodia: Starvation and Revolution', *Monthly Review*, New York, 1976 and John Baron, Paul Anthony, *Peace with Horror*, Hodder and Stoughton, London, 1977.
7. Chantou Boua and Ben Kiernan, 'Bureaucracy of death', *New Statesman*, 2 May 1980.

3. The People's Republic of Kampuchea

On 25 December 1978 a Vietnamese force of 120,000 men with armour and air support entered Kampuchea. Among these forces were a few thousand Khmer soldiers, some of whom were Kampucheans who had fled to Vietnam. On 7 January 1979, these troops reached Phnom Penh; three days later the establishment of the People's Republic of Kampuchea was declared by the People's Revolutionary Council. Heng Samrin, the leader of the Kampuchean National United Front of National Salvation (KNUFNS), became President.

The United Front had been founded a month earlier on 2 December 1978: its goal was to overthrow the Pol Pot regime and to 'establish a people's democratic regime . . . to make Kampuchea into a really peaceful, independent, neutral and non-aligned country advancing to socialism'. In addition to these general goals, the Front promised in its appeal to do away with the extremes of the Pol Pot period such as collective labour and collective meals as well as forced marriages, while emphasizing the right to return to former home areas, freedom of religion, the reuniting of families, and the creation of urban economies. A central goal was the creation of relations of friendship between Kampuchea and Vietnam.[1]

Already by 18 February, little over a month after the change of government, Vietnam's Prime Minister, Pham Van Dong, made a visit to Phnom Penh during which a treaty on friendship and co-operation between Kampuchea and Vietnam was signed. In content the treaty meant a military alliance in which both parties pledged all possible aid to the other if one were forced to defend the inviolability of its territory. Furthermore, it noted the 'traditional solidarity and fraternal friendship among the peoples of Kampuchea, Laos and Vietnam'. Vietnam had concluded a similar treaty with Laos in 1977. These friendship treaties formally confirmed the *de facto* situation in the region of Indo-China: a close-knit, three-nation military alliance had appeared under the leadership of Vietnam.

Vietnam had justified its military action in Kampuchea by pointing to the growing threat which China posed in the region of Indo-China. In practice the only ties to the outside world which Democratic Kampuchea had maintained were its relations with China. From there, it had received in addition to technical aid and expertise, increasing amounts of military aid. It was estimated that in 1978 there were 20,000 Chinese advisers in the country.[2] Also, for the Kampuchean Communist Party the Chinese Communists were ideologically the only outside reference group from which to draw support, although for the latter Kampuchean Communists represented the same kind of extreme leftism as that of the 'gang of four' which had been eliminated from China's leadership. China had, however, given its backing to Democratic Kampuchea for reasons of power politics: relations between China and Vietnam had gradually tensed to the point of near open war, a situation which had been crucially affected by the *rapprochement* between China and the United States.

For Vietnam, with its long and extremely vulnerable western border, relations with its two smaller neighbouring states came to be of strategic significance. The abrupt weakening of Vietnam's policy position and its attempt to avoid getting caught up in the cross-currents of geopolitics were weighty influnces in its opening of a large-scale military operation aimed at bringing down the government of Democratic Kampuchea. Escalating border clashes between Vietnam and Kampuchea had aggravated the situation to the point of near open war.[3] As early as May 1975, immediately after the capture of Phnom Penh and Saigon, the two armies of liberation had fallen into armed conflict; formally, the dispute concerned certain islands and some disagreements over the inland border.

The Kampucheans seized first the small island of Tho Chu and attacked Phu Quoc island; in retaliation the Vietnamese seized the island of Koh Way, after which it was possible to calm down the situation. Inland as well, there were border clashes in the so-called 'Parrot's Beak' area; the disputed border areas were not very large, altogether a matter of less than 70 km^2 of land and the delineation of the border off the coast, but the fact that it was not possible to settle the dispute immediately was an indication of the deep mistrust between the new governments of the two neighbouring countries. On the other hand, these areas have a certain strategic significance and importance in terms of natural resources. Promising off-shore oil finds have been made which had already previously affected the delineation of the border.

The border clashes escalated during 1977 (see Map 4); Democratic Kampuchea's internal pressures drove it to seek an external enemy. Troops of the Khmer Rouge encroached on villages in the Tay Ninh province of Vietnam and in the Mekong River delta. In April and September, large and extremely cruel attacks were carried out in the areas of Ha Tien and Tay Ninh; smaller attacks were also made on Thai villages. During November-December 1977 Vietnamese forces of about 50,000 men carried out a counterattack, 'taught a lesson', and penetrated for over a month as far as 40 km into the provinces of Takeo, Prey Veng and Svay Rieng. At the turn of the year, Phnom Penh broke off diplomatic relations between the two countries. The situation on the border did not, however, calm down. During the spring and summer of 1978 the Kampucheans made several attacks, which the Vietnamese returned. This state of affairs was further aggravated

BORDER CLASHES BETWEEN KAMPUCHEA AND VIETNAM 1975–78

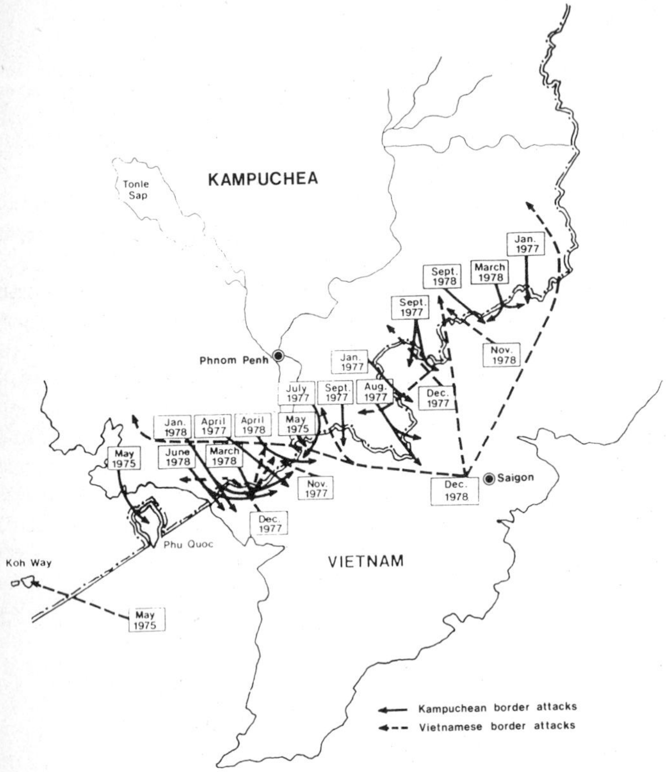

by Kampuchea's internal power struggle and most importantly by the rebel movement in the eastern provinces along the border with Vietnam and the brutal manner in which it was put down.

Following the founding of the United Front (KNUFNS) in December 1978 a new, more massive Vietnamese operation began, this time with the explicit aim of overthrowing the government in Phnom Penh.

Political Background of KNUFNS

The KNUFNS can be said to be comprised of three very different types of political orientation: the so-called Khmer-Vietminh, representatives of Khmer Rouge opposition groups and 'apolitical' representatives of the former intelligentsia.[4]

The primary and core group of the Front is made up of Kampuchean Communists who fled to Vietnam after the 1954 Geneva Conference and were in North Vietnam until the foundation of the National United Front of Kampuchea (FUNK) in 1970. Originally there were about 5,000 of them and they have traditionally been called 'Khmer-Vietminh' to distinguish them from the Khmer Rouge which remained inside Kampuchea. As early as the 1960s, differences over tactical viewpoints had led to confrontations between the different Communist wings which, following the founding of the FUNK, heated up into a power struggle for its leadership. The Khmer Rouge succeeded in turning the situation to its own advantage and at the end of 1972 began bloody internal purges. Several hundred Communists who had returned from Vietnam were killed in 1972-3. At the time there were clashes between the Khmer Rouge and Khmer-Vietminh supported Vietnamese units in Kampuchea. The remaining Khmer-Vieminh fled back to Vietnam and returned to their own country only when raised to power by the victorious Vietnamese army in 1979. The best known of the Khmer-Vietminh, and the most influential until his downfall in 1981, was Party leader and Prime Minister Pen Sovan.[5]

Internal power struggles within the Kampuchean Communist Party did not, however, end with the flight of elements sympathetic to the Vietnamese. The radical and intolerant line of action adopted by the Party leadership unavoidably led to opposition and rebellion. The Foreign Minister of Democratic Kampuchea, Ieng Sary, had admitted that during the years 1975-8 there were at least seven serious coup attempts. There were widespread rebellions in the province of Siem Reap and Prey Veng in 1977 ending in a massive rebel movement in eastern areas in May 1978. In line with its own policy, the Party leadership crushed resistance; in 1977-8 the Party's internal purges swept through the entire country, in practice down to every village.

Some of the rebels escaped into the jungles, and later from there into neighbouring countries. Almost all of the leaders of the opposition factions were, however, captured and thus those who escaped were mainly from second and third level cadres. For example, So Phim, who had led the rebel movement in the eastern areas was killed, but some local Committee leaders such as Mat Ly and Chea Sim, as well as Heng Samrin who had acted as the Secretary of the 4 division, escaped to Vietnam. It was on their names that the public face of the KNUFNS was constructed and thus the 1979 changeover of power received an authentic insurrectionist movement form.

The third political element in the KNUFNS is comprised of surviving public officials who served in the administrations of Sihanouk and Lon Nol as well as representatives of the intelligentsia or the Church. Some of them were recruited into the KNUFNS from among the 150,000 refugees who had fled to Vietnam and some who had remained in Kampuchea during the dissolution of Khmer Rouge power, that is if they had not moved into Thailand and tried to reach western countries from there. In terms of traditional orientation they were not leftists, rather mainly liberals and strongly nationalistic, but they joined the KNUFNS in order to oppose a rise to power by the Khmer Rouge. For example Deputy Foreign Minister Hornam Hong and Vandy Ka Onn, a member of the Council of State, both represent the previous liberal intelligentsia. One of the Deputy Speakers of the National Assembly, Tep Vong, is the head of the Buddhist Church, while Minister of Argriculture Kong Sam Ol, Education Minister Pen Navuth, and Minister for Culture Chheng Phon, who were named to their posts in 1981, were all members of the civil service during the period of Sihanouk and Lon Nol.

The core of the KNUFNS, however, is comprised of Khmer-Vietminh veterans: all key posts within the government are under their control. The Prime Minister was Pen Sovan, the Minister for Defence is Chan Si, the Minister of the Interior is Khang Sarin, the Minister for Planning is Chea Soth, the Minister for Public Finance is Chan Phin and the Minister for Industry is Keo Chanda, who are all Communists who spent more than 20 years in Vietnam. Similarly, the military leadership, Chiefs of the General Staff Soy Keo and Lim Nay, were educated at the military academy in Hanoi. The less important ministries dealing with social and cultural affairs have been left to technocrats, non-ideological representatives of the former civil service. Communists who defected from the Khmer Rouge to Vietnam have received the most typical 'show' positions in the top leadership: Heng Samrin is President, Hun Sen is Foreign Minister, and both Chea Sim and Mat Ly are Speakers of the National Assembly. Likewise, the list of the 18 members of the Central Committee of the People's Revolutionary Party made public in May 1981 contains 11 Khmer-Vietminh Communists and only five former Khmer Rouge.

The picture changes substantially upon examination of the administration and the construction of the Party on a regional or local level. The number of Vietnam-oriented Communists who were left after the purges of the Pol Pot period was so small that there are only just enough of them to fill the most important political positions on the provincial level.[6] The efficiency of the purges is well demonstrated, for example, by the average age of the current Party leadership, which for members of the Central Committee is as low as 46 (in Vietnam the average age of the members of the Central Committee is 68).

During the first phase, 1979-80, regional and local administration as well as the central administration had to be built to a great extent on the resources of the Vietnamese. When educated Khmers were found, they were recruited into the service of the state administration almost completely without regard to their previous political or social background. For many, the ability to read and do figures was the only qualification; in many cases even very crucial positions had to be filled with staff who were, in practice, incompetent; the job had to teach the worker. At the expense of administrative efficiency, direct participation by the Vietnamese was gradually reduced by 1983 to less than half the 1979 level.

The Security Situation

Even if the role of Vietnamese advisers in the administrative machinery of the country has sharply declined, the same cannot be said of the Vietnamese military presence. In 1983 there were still 150,000-180,000 Vietnamese soldiers in Kampuchea, whose presence was evident throughout the whole country. At its height, the number of Vietnamese troops was 200,000-220,000 men. The number of troops has gradually dropped and during the summer of 1982 Vietnam announced further reductions which have been estimated to consist of 20,000 to 30,000 soldiers.[7]

The Vietnamese arrival in December 1978 led to the collapse of the administrative machinery of Democratic Kampuchea in the most important areas of the country. The soldiers of the Khmer Rouge, the cadres and the members of the collectives who had more or less voluntarily followed them, fled in almost complete disorder before the quickly advancing Vietnamese. In each province those fleeing tried to make their way to certain chosen and partially stocked supply areas from where it was intended to undertake resistance.[8]

Having secured its hold on the cities and reinforced its army by seven to eight divisions following China's attack on its northern border in February-March, Vietnam began a new offensive in April 1979. In addition to the eastern and central regions, by the end of June the Vietnamese took complete control of the country's heavily populated south-western, western, and north-western regions, breaking up the Khmer Rouge supply areas and nests of resistance established there. In August a similar operation was directed towards the country's northern and north-eastern regions. By October 1979 practically the whole country was under the control of the Vietnamese and the government of the People's Republic of Kampuchea which had been established with their support.

The units of the Khmer Rouge and the part of the population that followed them made a completely chaotic retreat into the mountainous areas of western and northern Kampuchea from which they finally fled crushed and starving, across to Thailand. Without extensive support areas suitable for cultivation, the organization of resistance by the Khmer Rouge came to be based largely on international food and arms supplied by China.

Only at the settlements in the Phnom Malai highlands in the north-west, the Cardamom mountain passes in the west and the northern parts of the provinces of Siem Reap and Preah Vihear in the north of the country has it been possible to practise a limited degree of agriculture. These are the only areas in the country that can still be said to be under the control of the government of Democratic Kampuchea (see Map 5).

From the border camps and the supply areas located in the mountains, Khmer Rouge units have infiltrated into Kampuchea, usually in groups of 10-12 men, mining roads, organizing ambushes against military transports, and carrying out random attacks against Vietnamese bases. Usually the targets of these guerrilla patrols are not civilian settlements, but rather Vietnamese soldiers or representatives of the Phnom Penh government. The attack in June 1980 on a train travelling from Phnom Penh to Battambang which claimed some 200 civilian victims was more an exception than the rule. The railway line has been cut two or three times because of mine attacks. Also, many important roads, especially in the north and north-east have been closed to foreigners for security reasons. There is also a night-time curfew in the cities; in Phnom Penh, however, this is more or less symbolic. Since 1979 actual battles have not been fought anywhere except in the area along the border with Thailand. Heavily armed Vietnamese troops usually advance during the dry season and ease off in the summer with the beginning of the rainy season.

In 1980-1 there were battles in the remote Cardamom mountain area and in the northern provinces of Siem Reap and Preah Vihear. Traditionally the mountain tribes of the north-east have rebelled against the central government in Phnom Penh and the Khmer Rouge units who have infiltrated into the area have tried to encourage this resistance movement. However, major battles were fought in the area of Phnom Malai at the beginning of 1982 in which for the first time regular use of air forces was made against the guerrillas.

For the Vietnamese, the rear support provided to the guerrillas by Thailand has proven problematic in the conduct of the war. With the onset of major battle, the guerrillas usually flee across the border. This has repeatedly led to clashes between the Vietnamese and Thai armies. During the summer of 1980 a Vietnamese force of two divisions even seized for a few days the Nong Chan border camp and the Thai village of Non Mak Mun. These border clashes have further strained relations between Thailand and Vietnam.

Despite military operations in border areas, individual killings or ambushes, the security situation in Kampuchea is relatively stable. All of the heavily populated areas are under the control of the government of

Heng Samrin. The population is also relatively loyal to the current Phnom Penh government despite the fact that it came to power with the support of Vietnam. For the people the motives behind Vietnam's military operation are an altogether secondary question. Liberation from the rule of Pol Pot was crucial. As long as guerrilla action continues and as long as a return to power by the Khmer Rouge is seen even to the smallest degree as a realistic alternative, the population is in practice ready to give unanimous support to the presence of Vietnamese soldiers.

The Vietnamese are also aware of their position and have tried to assume as unseen a role as possible in order to avoid irritating the population. Soldiers are usually not seen in the city centres; their camps are located on the edge of settled areas, usually away from main roads. The bulk of the Vietnamese troops are in the actual battle areas in the unpopulated regions along the border with Thailand, or guarding strategically important buildings, bridges and dams. The military units have their own fields of crops attached to their camps and the soldiers have to subsist on the produce of these fields supplemented by supplies from Vietnam.[9] Food is scarce, but the soldiers are strictly forbidden to take foodstuffs from the local population, and in general the military leadership takes a dim view of contacts with the Kampucheans.[10]

The Vietnamese apparently do not want to endanger the strategic advantage they have gained in Kampuchea. The traditional mistrust between the Khmers and Vietnamese could be awakened too easily by an indifferent or dominating attitude; it is just this mistrust that the guerrilla movement attempts to feed and use to its own advantage.

Various surveillance and guard duties have been gradually turned over by the Vietnamese to the Khmers. Local troops of guards and militia units have been established in the villages and cities, and these are today mainly responsible for guarding bridges and the entrances to villages. The build-up of a national Khmer army had begun already in South Vietnam in 1978, although this did not happen on a broad scale until 1980 following the re-establishment of the general staff headquarters in Phnom Penh. The recruitment of soldiers has been on a volunteer basis, though in some provinces there has been an attempt at conscription. The strength of the army of the People's Republic of Kampuchea at the end of 1981 was estimated at 25,000 soldiers.[11] Up until now the army has carried out mainly guard duties, but in the areas of Pailin and Siem Reap some units have taken part in actual battles. Finding manpower has not been very difficult, rather the problem has been a lack of officers and arms. In addition to arms supplies it has been necessary to seek military training from abroad, and this has been provided especially by the Soviet Union along with Vietnam.

Population

On the basis of a census carried out in May 1981 the number of inhabitants in Kampuchea is estimated at approximately 6.7 million (see Table 3). This official count is relatively close to those estimates which representatives of international relief organizations have put forth as the actual population of the country. The last complete census was made in 1962; since then calculations of the number of inhabitants have been more or less rough estimates, the size of which has often been determined by political considerations. According to UN calculations the population in 1970 should have been around 7.1 million. On average the growth in population during the last years of peace (1965-70) was 2.8% per annum, so that if growth had continued normally the country's population at the beginning of the 1980s should have already reached over 9 million. The wars, executions, famines, lack of medical care, forced labour and stream of refugees, however, shattered the former expansion of population and in fact led to a decline in the number of inhabitants.

The first phase involved the expansion of the Vietnam War by the Americans into Kampuchea, during which time the population growth from 1970 – 5 fell to under 1% per annum. As the result of military operations an estimated 600,000 Kampucheans died.[12] It can be estimated that when the Khmer Rouge took power in 1975, the population of the country was approximately 7.3 million and a number of different observers concur with this figure.[13] In the summer of 1979 the Heng Samrin government announced that the population stood at 7.25 million when the Khmer Rouge came to power. The same figure was arrived at by the United States Central Intelligence Agency, the CIA, in its report on population development in Kampuchea during the 1970s.

The period of rule by the Khmer Rouge came to mean a new era of tragedy for the Kampucheans. Figures and estimates of the number of dead during the Pol Pot period are vague or are based on considerations of political expediency. Before the overthrow of the Pol Pot regime, generally two million victims were spoken of. Soon after the new government came to power in Phnom Penh it announced that 'the Pol Pot–Ieng Sary genocidal clique' had killed 3 million people. On 3 July 1979, in an appeal to the international community, the Foreign Ministry of the Republic of Kampuchea announced that during the Khmer Rouge period the country's population had fallen from 7.25 million to 4 million.

The population figure of 6.7 million arrived at in the 1981 census, however, indicated a smaller number of victims during the Pol Pot period than was previously suggested. By exaggerating the number of those who fell victim, the desire was to convince at first the international community of 'Pol Pot's policy of genocide' and thus justify the actions by Vietnam. Later, in 1981, the Phnom Penh government no longer needed to underestimate the size of the population because it had already become established practice to speak of millions of victims in examinations of the period of Pol Pot.

Table 3
Population Statistics for 1981

Provinces	*Population (thousands)*	*Active population (thousands)*	*National minorities (thousands)*	*Intellectuals*	*Monks*	*Villages*	*Solidarity groups*
Lowland provinces	3,954	1,851	120.2	7,220	3,610	6,803	53,620
Phnom Penh	329	155	13.1	2,160	90	77	1,300
Kandal	720	344	—	1,530	610	1,193	7,780
Kompong Cham	1,070	479	104.8	2,420	1,050	1,590	15,650
Svay Rieng	292	134	—	1,090	330	665	5,036
Prey Veng	672	307	0.4	—	540	1,116	10,664
Takeo	531	263	1.9	—	900	1,043	8,813
Kompong Speu	340	169	—	20	90	1,119	4,377
Tonle Sap provinces	1,971	949	17.0	2,120	980	3,353	27,497
Kompong Thom	379	179	8.7	1,190	220	674	5,147
Siem Reap	477	228	0.8	370	190	927	5,968
Battambang	719	341	2.7	310	460	939	9,729
Pursat	175	89	4.8	250	50	359	2,633
Kompong Chhnang	221	112	—	—	60	454	4,020
Coastal provinces	432	202	18.8	520	290	616	5,483
Kompong Som town	53	25	4.6	520	40	54	520
Kampot	354	165	10.2	—	230	456	4,632
Koh Kong	25	12	4.0	—	20	106	331
Mountain provinces	327	133	33.1	320	50	792	9,112
Preah Vihear	70	32	—	—	10	218	698
Stung Treng	39	19	—	300	10	115	5,663
Ratanakiri	45	23	—	—	—	171	453
Mondolkiri	16	9	12.7	—	—	55	161
Kratie	157	70	20.4	20	30	233	2,137
Total	*6,684*	*3,135*	*189.1*	*10,180*	*4,930*	*11,564*	*95,712*

Sources: Ministry for Planning and the Exhibition of Permanent Achievements, People's Republic of Kampuchea.

Furthermore, in order to optimize international food aid, the size of the population had rather to be overestimated. Apparently the Phnom Penh government had difficulties in making even a rough estimate of the population in 1979-80 because of the state of war and the massive movements of people. The population of Kampuchea also increased with the return of nearly 400,000 refugees during 1979-81.

The system of administration of the Khmer Rouge was based on the use of open force. Realistic estimates of the number of people who died as victims of executions range between 75,000-150,000.[14] Representatives of the government of Democratic Kampuchea have also admitted that 'some executions could not be avoided following the liberation of 1975' and that 'outsiders constantly want to inquire about those 5-10% of the Kampucheans who did well before the revolution instead of being interested in the fate of the poor masses'.[15]

Those who were the targets of direct execution, however, form but one part of all the human victims of the social experiment by the Khmer Rouge. The complete emptying of the cities within a couple of days immediately following the change of power on 17 April 1975 proved fatal for many thou-

MILITARY SITUATION IN KAMPUCHEA 1982

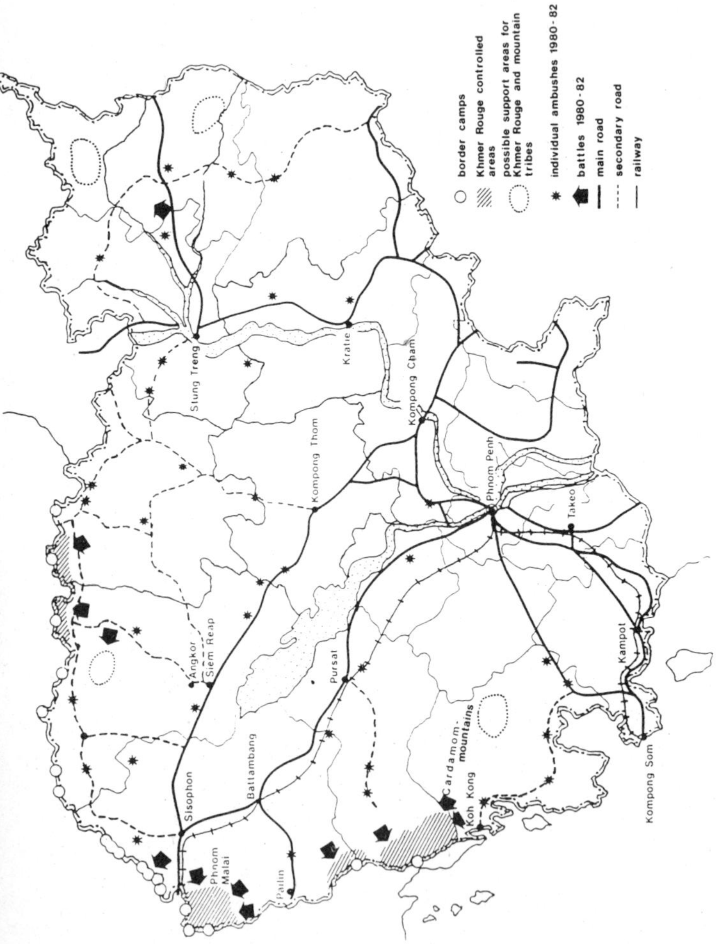

sands of sick people, old people and small children. Even representatives of the Democratic Kampuchea government admitted afterwards that the evacuation of Phnom Penh with its population of 3 million demanded some 2,000-3,000 deaths.[16]

Approximately two-thirds of Kampucheans were targets of the population transfers which were carried out in different contexts and in various parts of the country. People were forced to move on foot dozens and even hundreds of kilometres, which for many meant death. Forced labour on the agricultural communes was too much for many, and some of the transferred population suffered from malnutrition. Health care services were primitive and there was a lack of medicines, as a result of which it was not possible to give the sick proper care, and infant mortality rose sharply. The near-continuous warfare with neighbouring countries which began in 1977 also claimed victims.

It can be estimated that within four years, altogether nearly one million people died in Democratic Kampuchea. This figure has been reached with the calculations which follow: the population of Kampuchea in 1975 has been estimated at 7.3 million; if the natural growth in the population (births and natural deaths) is assumed to have stayed at the level of the 1960s, i.e. 2.8%, or to have slightly declined, the total population of the country in 1981 would have been about 8.3-8.5 million. According to the census carried out in May 1982, however, it was only 6.7 million. To this must be added the more than 300,000 refugees in Thailand, the over 100,000 refugees who had moved to western countries, and the some 250,000 Viet-Khmers who had settled permanently in Vietnam after 1975. In this way the figure of 7.4 million is arrived at, which is the total number of Khmers today living in Kampuchea and abroad. Thus it can be estimated that approximately one million people died during the period of Pol Pot. On the other hand, if one assumes that the natural growth in population of 2.8% fell during 1975-9 – which is quite probable – then the number of people who died during the period of Pol Pot would have been lower than one million.[17]

Losses were especially high among those 4-5 million inhabitants who had formerly lived in the cities and other areas under the control of the Lon Nol government. In contrast, the some 2.5-3 million people who lived in Khmer Rouge-controlled rural areas before the revolution did not suffer nearly as much under the Pol Pot administration. The number of dead in this group was perhaps a few per cent, most of whom lost their lives in Party purges and as a result of military operations.

The entry of Vietnamese troops in 1978 and the resulting flood of refugees and food shortages were the final tribulations. The number of dead that resulted from warfare and famine did not, however, exceed a few tens of thousands because the food crisis, which at first seemed to be very serious, did not prove overwhelming. It was possible to stave off the crisis with the help of international aid, first from Vietnam and later from elsewhere.

Examining the whole of the decade of the 1970s shows that the total loss in Kampuchea's population including refugees amounted to nearly two million people.[18] This means a loss of almost 30% of the entire population.

Such sharp changes cannot be imperceptible as problematic special features of the current population structure. First of all, the current population has an exceptionally heavy imbalance in the high number of women because the wars and executions took their toll mainly among the male population. On the basis of samples it is estimated that women comprise about 60% of the total population, and for women over the age of 20 this may rise to as high as nearly 75%. Secondly, a significant feature of the age structure is the gap for children three to eight years of age (born 1974-9) which may be relatively only half of the number of children in slightly higher or lower age group. This is explained by the high rate of infant mortality and the drop in the birth-rate during the war years of the Lon Nol period and the period of Pol Pot. The high rate of infant mortality of the past decade is now being compensated for in that the natural growth in the population during 1981 was around 4.6-5.2% – one of the highest in the world.[19]

Changes have also taken place in the population base of Kampuchea: as late as during the 1960s, it was estimated that national minorities made up nearly 10% of the entire population. Mostly these were urban ethnic Vietnamese and Chinese as well as numerous isolated mountain tribes, the largest of which were the Islamic Chams. During the period of Pol Pot, and earlier of Lon Nol, the national minorities were persecuted, and in practice the whole population of a quarter of a million Viet-Khmers fled permanently to Vietnam. The Chams, whose unique little communities were broken up and who were the targets of an attempt at 'Khmerization' suffered especially. The number of Chams fell from some 200 thousand to under 50 thousand during the Pol Pot period.[20] Today national minorities account for approximately 3% of the population (see Table 3), the largest being the Chinese minority which formerly made up 5-6% of the population. Since 1981 some ethnic Vietnamese have returned to Kampuchea and moved mainly into Phnom Penh or their former fishing villages on Lake Tonle Sap.

Reconstruction

In 1979 the internal social pressures for change which had been created by Democratic Kampuchea's nearly four-year social experiment erupted. The collective farms of the countryside, where almost the whole population had lived, fell apart. Similarly the repressive administrative system, which had maintained social cohesion and which the Vietnamese were not able to replace immediately, crumbled.

The break with the old and the creation of the new at first took on an anarchic form. This was most clearly seen in the massive movements of the people. Perhaps even half of the population can be said to have moved during 1979. Many were trying to flee from the battles to safety; some fled to Thailand; for the greatest number, however, the goal was the search for their former homes; the cities, little by little, filled up. In principle, travel documents were mandatory and there were travel restrictions in force, but in practice these regulations were impossible to enforce. There was apparantly no systematic attempt to prevent the movements of the population.

The number of inhabitants of Phnom Penh has gradually risen; by 1982 it had increased to nearly half a million, but most of the inhabitants are newcomers. It is estimated that only about a third of the present residents of the capital lived there before 1975. At the beginning, the looting of empty houses was typical; the new residents chose dwellings at complete random. They lacked any connection with the area's earlier traditions, as a result of which the face of the cities has deteriorated, and the material resources to repair the cities have not been available.

The state of war, the disrupted economic infrastructure and the sudden dissolution of social structures were to lead to a serious food crisis. The 1978-9 harvest had not been completed when the Vietnamese arrived. During their retreat, the Khmer Rouge managed to take with them 20-30% of the rice harvest and about a third of the draught animals.[21] When they left, they tried to destroy the remainder of the harvest which had been gathered in. The country was threatened by famine; the food shortage hit especially hard the part of the population that had moved into the cities. The chaotic situation in the countryside during the summer of 1979 also prevented the normal planting of crops, with the result that the 1979-80 rice harvest was only about a third of the usual. In 1979 and 1980 a serious famine was avoided only because of international food aid.

The most important task of the new Phnom Penh government has been to get agricultural production started as soon as possible and to strive for self-sufficiency in foodstuffs. In terms of the potential for food production, Kampuchea is a rich country. Before 1970 it was in fact a net exporter of foodstuffs. At that time the area under rice cultivation was around 2.2 million hectares. Already in the summer of 1980 it was possible to plant 1.5 million hectares, which nearly satisfied the country's minimum requirements. The late onset of the monsoons in the summer of 1981, however, caused drought followed by flooding, making it possible to cultivate only 1.3 million hectares, which meant that Kampuchea contined to be dependent on international food aid.[22] By the end of the year 1982, 1.7 million hectares of ricefields had been planted. To satisfy the minimum of self-sufficiency – 12 kg of rice per person per month – requires that approximately 1.8 million hectares are harvested. This is based on the assumption that 0.3 million hectares can be harvested during the dry season.

Average agricultural productivity per hectare is only about two-thirds of that at the beginning of the 1970s. The greatest problem has been the lack of the means of production: two-thirds of the supply of draught animals were destroyed; there are enough tractors to cultivate only 60,000 hectares, which is equivalent to somewhat less than 4% of the total area of land under cultivation; there is a shortage of fertilizers and insecticides; irrigation systems are inefficient because of their primitive technical nature, even though it was specifically the construction of canals and an extensive irrigation network that was one of the most important goals of the Khmer Rouge period.[23]

The fish catch in 1981 was about 50,000 tons. Before the wars, at the beginning of the 1970s, annual catches averaged 125,000 tons of which a considerable portion was exported. Today the organization of the fishing industry is difficult because of the lack of boats and nets, and the fact that the majority of the Mekong River and Lake Tonle Sap fishermen belonged to Vietnamese or Cham minorities which were dispersed during the period of Pol Pot.

The year 1979 brought a fundamental change in the approach to agricultural production: the collective farms of the Pol Pot period, which had been based in practice on forced labour, were broken up. The new administration is aiming at socialized agricultural production, but it has adopted a relatively pragmatic and soft approach in order to maximize the level of production and to stabilize the situation in the countryside. Private ownership of land was not reintroduced, but the means of production – most importantly draught animals – are privately owned. Additionally each family has the right to a quarter-hectare private plot around its house. The rural population is organized into solidarity groups *(krom samaki)* of 10-15 families each, of which there are a total of some 95,000 in the country. Within the solidarity groups rice is cultivated jointly, but the entire harvest is divided among the families in accordance with each one's investment of labour; invalids, the old and children are assigned a certain portion of the harvest. Taxes are not levied, so the families can sell their excess produce to the state grain stores or on the private market. The price per kilogram paid by the state is nearly the same as the going market rate. A future goal is to form co-operatives out of the solidarity groups, but at present during the transition period the aim is to encourage individual initiative in order to maximize output.

Even though a successful beginning has been made at organizing agricultural production, the same cannot be said of the other sectors of the economy. The avowed goal of the government is socialist planning, but at the moment the markets are functioning on their own conditions. Despite the deficiences in the distribution of foodstuffs, there is no rationing. As regards food, the countryside is already beginning to be self-sufficient. In contrast, the needs of the urban population have almost completely been supplied by international aid.

Street peddling is kaleidoscopic and various small businesses and repair shops dominate the street scene. The black market flourishes; goods smuggled in from Thailand sell well despite their high prices. For example, rather common Honda light motorcycles cost approximately 20,000 riels (1,500 US dollars) on the black market, a sum equivalent to ten years' salary for a state civil servant. Similarly, a portable radio costs 3,000 riels (200 US dollars). Sisophon has become the centre of illicit trading and from there goods move throughout the country and on to Vietnam and the black markets of Saigon and Hanoi. Smuggled goods are usually not bought with riels, but rather with gold of which there is still relatively a lot in the country in various caches. Money was brought into use in the spring of 1980; up until then the medium of exchange in all trading was either gold or rice and to a smaller extent Thai baahts and Vietnamese dongs.

The new riel has retained its value relatively well despite the fact that the banking system is only now being built up and thus the currency is not backed by central bank reserves. Finance is otherwise so undeveloped that the state in 1982 has still not imposed any taxes. Thus the state has no budget of its own, but rather its activities are primarily financed by aid from outside. Salaries are partly paid in kind; civil servants, for example receive 16-20 kg of rice – depending on their position – at a subsidized price of one riel per kilogram as part of their salary. Rent is not paid on dwellings, nor is electricity billed. Formally dwellings are not owned by anyone, but are only under the supervision of the cities' block committees. The tasks of these committees are to supervise order, to unify the community of inhabitants and to organize the joint cleaning of the city and the dwellings on Sundays.

Salaries vary from 70 to 200 riels a month which, according to black market rates, is equal to 4-12 US dollars. The average earnings of a labourer are 90 riels, teachers' salaries range between 90 and 120 riels, a government minister's salary is 230 riels and President Heng Samrin's monthly earnings are 260 riels. Such low salaries have increased the attractiveness of more or less illegal opportunities for extra earnings. The degree of corruption in Kampuchea today is, however, relatively low. According to representatives of international aid organizations in Phnom Penh, as a result of the low level of corruption under the new government, the percentage of loss of international aid has remained exceptionally low. According to various estimates 90-95% of the aid has reached the intended receivers. The largest earnings are made in the private sector through trade and by supplying various services. Cycloped taxis earn more money than state civil servants and the country's really high incomes are to be found among the smugglers and various middlemen.

There is practically no industry in the country at all: in the wake of the Pol Pot period there were 60 functioning industrial plants, mainly light consumer good industries. It is difficult to keep these in operation because of the lack of spare parts and raw materials, but above all because of the lack of technical expertise. The infrastructure is being built up gradually: rail connections from Phnom Penh to Battambang and Kompong Som have been opened, but the trains run irregularly. Roads all over the country are badly damaged and unrepaired except for the main roads in the immediate vicinity of Phnom Penh – the road surfacing everywhere is broken; in contrast Kampuchea's small number of road vehicles are the most modern in the world. As a result of international aid operations during 1979-81 some 1,800 trucks and 700 jeeps and cars were brought into the country – this, however, is less than a sixth of the number of vehicles in the country in 1969. Communication links are being created: post and telecommunications have just started to function, but telex connections abroad are not in operation. Telephone lines have been opened within Phnom Penh, but the long-distance telephone network is not yet functioning. Electricity production is to be found only in the largest cities, Phnom Penh, Battambang, Siem Reap and Kompong Som; Phnom Penh uses 90% of the country's electricity and even there the supply is unreliable.

Foreign trade cannot be said to exist in the usual sense: imports consist mainly of aid shipments of food and medicine or machinery, equipment and spare parts received from the socialist countries; exports are only being started. Up to now the main export has been raw rubber sent to the Soviet Union and some other eastern European countries.

Before 1970 the area of rubber plantations in Kampuchea totalled 75,000 hectares. Today the potential area for use is around 50,000 hectares, of which only 8,000 hectares were utilized in 1981. One large problem is the lack of mechanization and of facilities for refining the sap. The Soviet Union has offered technical help in mechanizing the rubber plantations and in constructing rubber-refining facilities. Dried fish has been exported to neighbouring countries; Japan has bought small shipments of kapok, and cotton has been sold to Japan, Vietnam, Thailand and Tanzania.[24] The exports have been more in the nature of trial shipments. There are plans to follow Vietnam's lead by joining the socialist nations' Council for Mutual Economic Assistance, the CMEA (Comecon). Under the internal division of labour within the socialist community, Kampuchea's role would mainly be to produce various basic agricultural commodities. As regards rice, there are good chances of attaining the traditional position of a surplus producer. Raw rubber, tobacco and possibly cotton, as well as soybeans, maize and especially fish products may become other central export commodities.

At the moment, however, the emphasis in development is on reconstruction work and on increasing self-sufficiency: first place has been given to the development of agriculture. In the development of industry too emphasis has been laid on activities that support agriculture such as refining, the production of fertilizers and simple agricultural tools, and the construction of consumer industries aimed at satisfying the needs of the countryside. The next items on the list of priorities are the construction of the social infrastructure by the development of educational facilities and a health care system as well as improvements in electrical power distribution and transportation.[25]

The striving for self-sufficiency does not mean the isolation it meant during the period of the Khmer Rouge, but rather the goal is co-operation with the industrialized countries. The socialist countries have offered their help; in contrast, the western nations and the international aid organizations bound to them, for reasons of international politics, have been unwilling to expand co-operation from purely emergency aid in the direction of development projects. Under Kampuchea's current conditions, the building of a basic infrastructure can, however, be considered comparable to emergency aid in that without external help the nation's economy currently does not have the resources to function even passably.

Education

One of the greatest problems is the shortage of educated people. During the period of Pol Pot, repression fell relatively more heavily upon the educated: many died and many more tried to escape abroad. For example, of Kampuchea's 450 doctors before the war, only 50-55 were in the country in 1979. Over 200 doctors had, however, left the country already before 1975. Of those doctors remaining in 1979, some 20 have since left Kampuchea. Similarly, of the more than 20,000 teachers in the country at the beginning of the 1970s, only about 5,000 remain. Most of the teachers went with the flood of refugees to Thailand and attempted to reach third countries.[26]

A critical point in health care was passed when an essential improvement began in the food situation during 1980. People weakened by malnourishment suffered from anemia, dysentery, tuberculosis, malaria and various parasites. The number of medical personnel in the country was too small to even make a start at treating these people, not to mention the lack of medicine. Little by little with the help of international aid the situation has improved. There are 25 primitive hospitals operating in the country and some hundred health centres. The medical personnel are largely from abroad; similarly, medicines are bought in from outside. There are still problems however. The distribution of medicine to the country's health care facilities is logistically difficult, not to mention the problems involved in interpreting the instructions for medication from a dozen different countries. The training of health care personnel has begun – already in 1979 an institute for medical science staffed by teachers from socialist countries was established in Phnom Penh.

The development of the educational system has had to be started from the beginning. Illiteracy has climbed to 40% and the bulk of children 6-14 years of age lack any basic education. Now, nearly 80% of children of school age are in school; the emphasis is on the very lowest level in which over 97% of the pupils were enrolled in 1982 (see Table 4). It will perhaps not be until 1986-7 that all school beginners will be six year-olds. In adult education the first tasks have been a literacy campaign and the accomplishment of the lowest level of schooling.

This work has been started under very inadequate conditions. Presentable figures on the number of schools, teachers and pupils hide the barren truth: school buildings in many places are only temporary structures; classes of 70-80 children work on dirt floors without desks or sufficient school supplies; teachers have to teach two or three shifts (evening adult classes) a day; most teachers are without formal teacher-training; in many cases pupils from the upper classes teach those in the lower classes. There have been intensive short-term courses organized around the country to train teachers, and temporary teacher-training institutes have been established in the provinces. The programme of instruction of the lower levels consists mainly of the Khmer language and basic mathematics, moral education, history, geography and practical training related to farming.

Table 4
Development of the Educational System 1979-82

	1979-80	*1980-81*	*1981-82*
Kindergartens (pre-school 3-5 years)			
Kindergartens	96	211	402[a]
Classes	230	470	801
Children	8,229	15,077	23,021
Teachers	267	630	1,200[a]
Level 1 (4 grades)			
Schools	5,290	4,334[b]	3,521[b]
Classes	17,761	27,217	31,909
Pupils	947,317	1,328,053	1,508,985
Teachers	21,605	30,316	37,000[a]
Level II (3 grades)			
Schools	14	62	108
Classes	101	394	930
Pupils	5,104	17,331	39,434
Teachers	206	671	1,600[a]
Level III (3 grades)			
Schools	1	2	5
Classes	7	14	34
Pupils	301	555	1,521
Teachers	20	28	78[a]
Higher education			
Teacher-Training Institute (ENS)	—	206	422
Institute of Technology (ITSAKS)	—	—	220
Vocational School (Tuk Thla)	—	—	105
Language School (Khmer, Vietnamese, Russian)	—	142	207
Institute of Medical Science	—	—	800
Institute of Agriculture	—	—	1,000
Students abroad	—	305	597
Adult education[c]			
Classes	459	15,593	17,522
Pupils	13,778	491,625	544,408
Teachers	537	18,525	19,484

a. Planned
b. Regrouping of schools
c. Literary programme and level I and level II schooling
Source: Ministry of Education, People's Republic of Kampuchea.

Foreign language studies in Russian and Vietnamese are begun at the second and third levels. Getting language studies underway, especially Russian studies, has proved problematic because of the shortage of qualified teachers; there is no intention of including the former dominant foreign language, French, nor the somewhat less important English in the elementary school syllabus.

At the moment there are no universities in Kampuchea, nor any unified system of higher education. Institutes in various individual fields have been established with the support of mainly the socialist countries: the Soviet Union, for example, has financed and provided teachers for an institute of technology and an institute of agriculture in Phnom Penh. In order to get university level training Kampucheans must go abroad: over 900 students have gone abroad to universities and technical institutes in socialist countries – 600 of these students are studying in the Soviet Union.[27]

Traditionally, the Buddhist monks have held the main responsibility for primary education in the country: during the period of Democratic Kampuchea the practice of religion, however, was banned and monasticism abolished.[28] Before 1975 there were 80,000 monks in the country, of whom an estimated 50,000 have died. Also the pagodas suffered from systematic destruction: of the 2,400 temples in the country, 95% were destroyed. Since 1979 the Buddhist community has been able to reorganize: in 1982 there were nearly 5,000 monks and 740 pagodas had been fairly well repaired.[29] The re-established pagoda schools, however, have lost their former independence and are integrated into the national system of education.

The Angkor temple area, which is of immense value in terms of the entire world's cultural history, survived the upheavals of the 1970s. The most visible damage has been suffered by the some 3,000 different pictures and sculptures of the Buddha in the temple of Angkor Wat. There are only 16 still left undamaged. The remainder have either been toppled over or the heads have been broken off in testimony of the opposition to religion of the Pol Pot period. The national museum in Phnom Penh and the Royal Palace with its sacred silver pagoda have been relatively well preserved. On the other hand, of the some 100,000 volumes which were in the national library, only 30,000 remain.[30] The library was not systematically destroyed or censored, but rather the collection suffered from neglect. The use value of books had changed: they were not read, but used for lighting fires and for fuel: the library still does not function. The spread of information is otherwise limited – for example there is no daily press, though there are three weekly journals which appear in Phnom Penh.

During 1981 Kampuchea's public political system of administration was also reconstructed. Elections for local committees were held in March and on 1 May representatives were elected to the 117 seat National Assembly; the official level of voter turnout was 98%. Representatives of groupings other than the Communists were urged to become candidates. The KNUFNS Front nominated the candidates so that in each voting district there were a few more names on the list than the number of seats assigned to the district. Thus the voters had the opportunity to choose from the list their favourites, or more likely drop from the list their least favourite candidates; 81 of the 117 members elected to the National Assembly are members of the Communist Party. In June the National Assembly approved a constitution for the country and named the Council of Ministers to the government. The most important political happening was the coming out into public of the Kampuchean People's Revolutionary Party (Communist Party) at its fourth Party Congress (first public meeting) in May. The number of full Party members is estimated to be 160 and together with candidates for membership the entire Party is comprised of only some 600-700 individuals – which says something about how thin a layer the local ruling political élite is.[31]

Despite the narrow scope of the elite and the continuing hostilities, the policies the government has practised have been relatively lax and adaptable to the extraordinary conditions. According to the Constitution the goal is to progress gradually toward socialism, but in practice economic and social policy have been more in the nature of a liberalism based on market forces and individual initiative. At least for the time being there do not exist the material and administrative resources any more than the psychological possibilities for the development of a system of centralized state regulation. The population reacts with pent up anger to public management and planning, and in general the concept of socialism is difficult to use as a basis for policy after the 'socialist' social experiment of the Pol Pot period. Thus, the legitimacy of the Heng Samrin administration is based far more on the repulsiveness of the former regime than on the alternative policies it has offered.

The new government has a long way to go in order to convince the people of the legitimacy of the line it has chosen and the need for the building of socialism. In this respect the lax, gradually advancing and tolerant attitude adopted has been the only workable point of departure. Political opponents are much rather 're-educated' than violently eliminated. Estimates of the number of political prisoners in this country – which is in a state of war-range from only 1,000-3,000.[32] Imprisoned Khmer Rouge are treated with surprising tolerance: some have been sentenced to long terms of imprisonment, but many have been returned to their home villages. There have been no public executions and there have been no reports of torture. On the other hand some known Khmer Rouge may have been the targets of personal revenge.[33]

Notes

1. 'Declaration of the National United Front for the Salvation of Kampuchea', NUFSK Information Service, January 1979.
2. Richard Dudman, 'Travel report to Kampuchea', *Congressional Record-Senate*, 18 January 1979.
3. The main documents in which Vietnamese positions about the conflict with Democratic Kampuchea have been presented are: *The Vietnam–Kampuchea Conflict (A Historical Record)*, Hanoi, 1979; *War Crimes of the Pol Pot and Chinese troops in Vietnam*, Hanoi, 1979; and *Kampuchea Dossiers* I, II, III, Hanoi 1978-9.

The view of Democratic Kampuchea has been presented in: *Black Paper: Facts and Evidences of the Acts of Aggression and Annexation of Vietnam against Kampuchea*, Ministry of Foreign Affairs, Phnom Penh, 1978.

See also Serge Thion, 'The integratitude of crocodiles', *Bulletin of Concerned Asian Scholars*, Vol.12, No.4, 1980; Michael Vickery, op.cit.; Anthony Barnett, 'Inter-Communist Conflicts and Vietnam', *Bulletin of Concerned Asian Scholars*, Vol.11, No.4, 1979; Stephen Heder, 'The Kampuchean–Vietnamese Conflict', *South-East Asian Affairs 1979*, Singapore, 1979 and Stephen Heder, 'Origins of the Conflict', *Southeast Asia Chronicle*, No.64.

4. See Stephen R. Heder, 'From Pol Pot to Pen Sovan to the Villages', Institute of Asian Studies, Bangkok, mimeo, 1980.
5. For background factors to the overthrow of Pen Sovan see Nayan Chanda, 'Now a non-person', *Far Eastern Economic Review*, 18 December 1981 and Ben Kiernan, 'The New Political Structure in Kampuchea', *Dyason House Papers*, Australian Institute of International Affairs, Vol.8, No.2, December 1981.
6. Nayan Chanda, 'The survivors' party', *Far Eastern Economic Review*, 12 June 1981.
7. See Della Denman, 'Withdrawal symptoms', *Far Eastern Economic Review*, 16 July 1982.
8. Stephen Heder, 'Kampuchean Occupation and Resistance', *Asian Studies Monographs* No.27, Institute of Asian Studies, Chulalongkorn University, Bangkok, January 1980.
9. In 1979 many observers, basing their views mainly on reports from refugees, speculated that as a result of their military operation the Vietnamese were attempting to ease their own difficult food supply situation at the expense of the Kampucheans. Claims were especially made that part of the international food relief delivered to Phnom Penh was either shipped to Vietnam or consumed by Vietnamese troops. See for example William Shawcross, 'The End of Cambodia', *The New York Review of Books*, No.21-22, 24 January 1980 as well as Stephen R. Heder, op.cit. In interviews with representatives of international relief organizations in Phnom Penh in February 1982 the delegation of the Kampuchea Inquiry Commission did not hear of a single verifiable instance of the Vietnamese taking emergency relief to Kampuchea. Shawcross re-evaluated his claims following a visit to Kampuchea, see William Shawcross, 'In a Grim Country', *The New York Review of Books*, 24 September 1981.
10. See Paul Quinn-Judge, 'View from the Front', *Far Eastern Economic Review*, 9 April 1982.
11. Timothy Carney, 'Kampuchea in 1981: Fragile Stalemate', *Asian Survey*, Vol.XXII, No.1, January 1982.
12. Estimates of the victims of military operations during the years 1970-5 vary: according to Democratic Kampuchea the number of dead was 600,000 - 800,000. United States estimates range from 600,000 to 700,000 while according to Prince Sihanouk the number of dead was around 600,000.
13. A number of different observers concur with the estimate of 7.3 million for the population of Kampuchea in 1975. The Heng Samrin government announced in the summer of 1979 that the population was 7.25 million at the time that the Khmer Rouge came to power. The same figure was reached also in a report by

the United States intelligence agency, the CIA, dealing with population development in Kampuchea during the 1970s. Central Intelligence Agency, National Foreign Assessment Center, 'Kampuchea: A Demographic Catastrophe', Washington, May 1980.

14. Kurt Jansson who acted as UNICEF's special representative in Kampuchea 1980-1 gave the Kampuchea Inquiry Commission an estimate of the number of people executed during the Pol Pot period at approximately 70,000 - 100,000.
15. See report by Richard Dudman on his December 1978 visit to Kampuchea, *Congressional Record-Senate*, 18 January 1979, and Nayan Chanda, 'Interview with Ieng Sary', *Far Eastern Economic Review*, 22 June 1979.
16. Interview with Ieng Sary, *Der Spiegel*, No.20, 1977. See also 'Human Rights of Cambodia', Hearing before the Subcommittee on International Organizations of the Committee on International Relations, House of Representatives, 95th Congress, Washington, July 1977.
17. If the natural growth in population was during 1975-9, for example, 1.5% (and during 1980-1 around 4%) then the total population in the spring of 1981 would have been approximately 8.1 million. This would mean that the number of people who died during the period of Pol Pot would have been approximately 700,000.
18. Compare with CIA, op. cit., May 1980, which estimates total population losses during the 1970s at 2.7 million. Michael Vickery has criticized the CIA report for underestimating the losses during the Pol Pot regime's last years and for exaggerating the losses under the Heng Samrin government. Michael Vickery, 'Kampuchean Demography – Cooking the Books', mimeo, Canberra, November 1980.
19. Chantou Boua, *Women in Kampuchea*, UNICEF, Bangkok, August 1981. Michael Richardson, 'The 10-child Family', *Far Eastern Economic Review*, January 1982, and Frances Starner, 'Born out of Sorrow, a National Baby Boom', *Asiaweek*, 19 June 1981.
20. Frances Starner, 'The Chams: Muslims the World Forgot', *Asiaweek*, 21 November 1980, and Vu Can, 'The Community of Surviving Muslims', *Vietnam Courier*, No.4, 1982.
21. Stephen R. Heder, op. cit.
22. FAO, Special Programme secretariat in Phnom Penh. See also, 'FAO Food and Agriculture Assessment Mission to Kampuchea, 23 Oct. - 5 Nov. 1981, 'Report by the Inter-Agency Working Group on Kampuchea', New York, November 1981.
23. During the period of Pol Pot, canals and dikes were constructed exclusively with human labour. Some of the larger dike projects have proved unusable and have even disintegrated because of the lack of sufficient expertise and technical aids. It is estimated that about 80% of the irrigation systems constructed during the period of Pol Pot are in need of repairs or reconstruction. The best irrigation networks along the Chinit River in Kompong Thom, the Pursat River in Pursat and the Slako River in Takeo have been, however, useable as such. Interview with the head of the Ministry for Planning of the People's Republic of Kampuchea, Keo Samuth.
24. Japan was the first Western nation to open trade relations with the People's Republic of Kampuchea; in August 1980 a trade agreement was concluded between the Japan–Cambodia Trade Association and the Export–Import

Corporation of Cambodia.

25. Statements to the Kampuchea Inquiry Commission by the Ministries for Planning and Agriculture of the People's Republic of Kampuchea.
26. Information from the Ministry of Education, People's Republic of Kampuchea, as well as Serge Thion and Michael Vickery, 'Cambodia, Background and Issues', Church World Service, Kampuchea Programme, Phnom Penh, September 1981.
27. Information supplied to the Kampuchea Inquiry Commission by the Ministry of Education, People's Republic of Kampuchea.
28. Under the Constitution of Democratic Kampuchea freedom of religion was guaranteed, but all reactionary religions were banned. In practice all religions were considered reactionary.
29. Statement by the head of the Buddist Church, Tep Vong, to the Kampuchea Inquiry Commission in February 1982.
30. In March 1982 the National Library's collection consisted of a disorganized mass of various written material. New works in evidence were collections of Lenin's writing, APN file series, Dimitrov's biographies and Vietnamese material. The old collections included works from the period of French rule as well as for example USIS material from the 1950s and 1960s such as works of Wurmbrandt and CIA-produced anti-communist literature.
31. Timothy Carney, op. cit., 1982.
32. There are an estimated 5,000 prisoners in Kampuchea, half of whom may have been imprisoned for political reasons; cf., Ben Kiernan, op.cit., 1981.
33. Stephen Heder, 'Departures from Democratic Kampuchea – Control Zones', mimeo for Seminar Vietnam, Indochina and Southeast Asia: into the 80's, Institute of Social Studies, The Hague, October 1980.

4. Refugees and Opposition Movements

The most immediate reflection of wars and internal upheaveals are the people who flee from their homes. In the Kampuchea of the 1970s an estimated 70-80% of the population were at some time either refugees or subject to transfer, some of them more than once. At the beginning of the decade hundreds of thousands of people fled from the countryside into the cities to escape bombing by the Americans. This was followed by the repression of the Khmer Rouge period and transfers of population which led to a gradually increasing flow of refugees into neighbouring countries. During the years 1975-8, an estimated 150,000 Khmers fled to Vietnam and an estimated 50,000 to Thailand. Most of the latter have moved on to third countries (see Table 5). Finally, the Vietnamese troops at the end of the decade and the fall of the Pol Pot regime created a new, massive flood of refugees.

In the spring of 1979, Kampuchean refugees began crossing into Thailand: by June there were 17,000 UNHCR holding centres and another estimated 40,000 in the border zone between Thailand and Kampuchea. These first refugees were typically former members of the urban middle class, shopkeepers, teachers and civil servants who immediately tried to escape abroad as soon as the forced labour system of the collective farms collapsed. They were often carrying with them their few possessions of jewelry and objects of gold.

At first Thai officials tried to turn the newcomers back, even by means of violently enforced transfers. Thus, many did not reach the UN controlled holding centres, but rather were forced to seek safety in the camps of various smugglers, criminals and right-wing guerrilla movements in the border area. Already in the 1950s and 1960s these numerous little camps had been bases for right-wing Khmer Serei groups which opposed Prince Sihanouk and supported the military coup of Lon Nol.

It was from here that the Thai-supported wing of the Khmer Issarak movement had earlier mounted opposition against the French. The designation 'Khmer Serei' (Free Khmer) during the 1960s came to be used as a term for all of the various right-wing guerrilla groups that have traditionally operated in the border zone. They are mainly in the nature of bands of armed bandits, or smugglers and spies. During the time of the Pol Pot

Table 5
Khmer Refugees 1975-81

Total refugees (1975-81)		**850,000**
of whom fled to:		
Vietnam		150,000
Thailand 1975-78		50,000
Thailand 1979-81		630,000
Laos		20,000
Returnees to Kampuchea following March 1979 from:		
Vietnam		130,000
Thailand		234,000
Laos		20,000
Total		*384,000*
Resettled in the following provinces:		
Battambang	120,000	
Siem Reap	79,000	
Prey Veng	68,000	
Takeo	45,000	
Svay Rieng	72,000	
Total	*384,000*	
Moved to third countries 1975-79		72,000
Moved to third countries 1980-81		44,000
Total		*116,000*
Final destination country:		
United States	74,200	
France	21,400	
Canada	5,800	
Australia	4,100	
Switzerland	1,300	
New Zealand	1,200	
Federal Republic of Germany	800	
Belgium	600	
Other	6,600	
Total	*116,000*	
Remaining refugees (January 1982) in:		
Vietnam	Ethnic Chinese	20,000
Thailand		330,000
Total		*350,000*

Sources: UNHCR, Regional Office for Western South Asia, Bangkok; UNHCR, Special Programme Unit, Phnom Penh; Royal Thai Army, Task Force 80, Aranyaprathet.

regime, the Khmer Serei groups were unable to rise to any political or military significance, even though they were joined by officers and soldiers of Lon Nol's army who had escaped from Kampuchea. They remained small and divided: not until 1979 did the flow of refugees make an essential change in the situation.

In September-October 1979 there began a massive flood of refugees in which nearly half a million ill and starving people sought safety along the border with Thailand. These were the remains of the army and cadres of the Khmer Rouge accompanied by a part of the population that had followed more or less voluntarily. Vietnamese troops had broken up the support areas planned by the Khmer Rouge inside Kampuchea and had driven these people into the uninhabitable mountain and jungle areas. The Khmer Rouge, however, tried desperately to keep these people under their control by preventing their escape to the Vietnamese side or to Thailand. It was only in the extreme situation when according to some estimates a quarter of the civilian population had died of hunger, sickness or wounds that people finally were able to flee to Thailand. The Khmer Rouge system of control completely collapsed.

International aid organizations had begun activities to help the Khmer refugees in September. In October 1979, at the time of the largest influx of refugees, the Thai government unexpectedly changed its policy on refugees and opened the border. Large holding centres, the most important being the Khao I Dang, Kamput, Mairut and Sakaeo centres, were established under the management of UNHCR. The largest holding centre, Khao I Dang, was laid out for 300,000 refugees. It was imagined that all of the refugees were as starving and weak as those who had been under Khmer Rouge control and it was thought that the food supply situation inside Kampuchea was completely catastrophic. The Thai government calculated that the number of refugees could rise to one million or even two million, which it was believed would seriously rock the new Phnom Penh government. The Kampucheans did not, however, 'vote with their feet' to the extent that had been figured. The number of refugees in the Khao I Dang centre at its greatest rose to no more than 130,000. The refugees began to be a burden for Thailand itself, particularly when it turned out that the Western countries were not prepared to accept as many Khmer refugees as had been expected.

About 300,000 refugees who had come with the Khmer Rouge were housed at the Sakaeo centre which is located 60 km inside the Thai border. In the summer of 1980 the centre was closed and its residents were transferred either to the Khao I Dang centre or to the new Ban Kaeng centre which was established near Sakaeo. In this way an attempt was made to break up the internal system of control by the Khmer Rouge which had appeared in the centre and to end the possibilities for recruiting soldiers. The government of Thailand has repeatedly pressured the international aid organizations to change the locations of their holding centres. Thus the organizations have had to build a new refugee camp while more often than not the Thai army has taken over the old camp with its well developed infrastructure.

In January 1980 Thailand closed its border and refugees were directed into camps on the frontier. There are more than 20 of these border camps and today they house over 200,000 refugees (see Table 6 and Map 7). During 1979-80 various political and military organizations fought among themselves for the control and supervision of these camps. The borderline is not completely undisputed and Thailand claims that the camps are on the Kampuchean side. The background to this can be seen as an attempt to gradually close all of the UNHCR supervised holding centres and transfer some 100,000 refugees still in them to the 'Kampuchean side'[1] – people moved back into their homeland lose their status as refugees and are no longer under international supervision through the auspices of UNHCR.

On the other hand, the border camps are in practice bases controlled by the Kampuchean opposition movements. Thus Thailand is apparently attempting to create on its frontier some kind of buffer zone composed of Khmer refugees from whom political and military movements opposed to the Phnom Penh government can recruit new forces, rather than to create the possibilities for the refugees to return to their homes, which is the goal of the UNHCR refugee policy.[2] According to UNHCR representatives Thailand's policy can be characterized as relocation rather than repatriation which is what UNHCR itself is aiming at. The relocation programme is maintaining instability in the area farther than facilitating the search for a lasting solution.

There have been numerous cases of the Thai army violating the generally accepted international rights of refugees by forcibly moving people from UNHCR holding centres to border camps. It is estimated that between the end of 1980 and the beginning of 1982, 20,000 refugees were subject to this kind of 'illegal' transfer. Similarly, when UNHCR tried to move 9,000 refugees over the border into Kampuchea at the end of 1980, troops of the opposition movement, with indirect support from the Thai army, attacked the returnees, resulting in the deaths of several dozen. Since then, UNHCR has not tried to carry out its repatriation programme via the border.

The physical conditions for life in the refugee camps have been relatively good: the Kampuchean refugees live better than their countrymen in Kampuchea or the Thai villagers in the vicinity: the supply of food is regular and relatively balanced; the hospital are of a relatively high standard and the schools are significantly better supplied than inside Kampuchea. This has been achieved as a result of exceptionally broad and efficient international aid activities. The Kampucheans are perhaps the best cared for refugees in the whole areas of Asia and Africa.[3] In order to reduce the incongruity between the refugees and the local Thai population the international aid organizations have begun a programme under which food and medical aid are provided for 80,000-120,000 inhabitants of Thai affected villages.

The United Nations with its special organizations created the framework for refugee care and has taken responsibility for the distribution of food. Voluntary private relief organizations in turn have taken care of education,

Table 6
Khmer Refugee Camps in Thailand, February 1982

UNHCR Holding Centres				
		population		
Khao I Dang		43,000		
Ban Kaeng (Sakaeo II)		24,500		
Kamput		14,500		
Phanat Nikhom (transit centre)		9,500		
Lumpuk (refugees 1975-78)		2,000		
Total			*93,500*	
Border Camps				
Northern zone (WFP, RTA)				
	(code)			*Controlling movement*
Nam Yun	(N1)	2,500		KPNLF
Chong Chom (O'Smach)	(N2)	2,000		Moulinaka
Khun Han	(N3)	1,000		Khmer Rouge
O'Bok	(N4)	1,500		KPNLF
Ban Bara Nae (O'Ksach)	(N5)	6,000		Moulinaka
Paet Um (Smrong Kiat)	(N6)	14,000		Khmer Rouge
Naeng Mut	(N7)	300		Khmer Rouge
Total			*27,300*	
Ban Cha Rat	(N8)	(no intern. food aid)	10,000	Khmer Rouge
Central zone (WFP, UNBRO)				
Nong Pru	(NW1A)	8,000		Khmer Rouge
Tap Prik	(NW1B)	8,000		Khmer Rouge
Ban Sangae	(NW2)	11,000		KPNLF
Nong Samet	(NW3)	44,500		KPNLF
Phnom Chat	(NW4)	13,000		Khmer Rouge
Kok Tahan	(NW4A)	7,000		Khmer Rouge
Nong Chan	(NW7)	36,500		KPNLF and Moulinaka 4000
Camp 82 (Vietnamese)		1,000		
Total			*129,000*	
Khao Din	(NW6)	(no intern. food aid)	25,000	Khmer Rouge
Southern zone (WFP, RTA)				
Sok Sann (Kraduk Chan)	(S2)	9,000		KPNLF
Borai	(S3)	19,000		Khmer Rouge
Ta Luen	(S4)	17,000		Khmer Rouge
Total			*45,000*	
Khao Larn (Thai Red Cross)			200	
Total refugees			**330,000**	
of which:				
in Khmer Rouge controlled camps			122,000	
in KPLNF camps			101,000	
in Moulinaka camps			12,000	

Sources: UNHCR, Regional Office for Southern Asia, Bangkok; UNBRO Office, Aranyaprathet; Royal Thai Army, Task Force 80, Aranyaprathet.

WFP = World Food Programme
RTA = Royal Thai Army
UNBRO = United Nations Border Relief Operation

health services and the agricultural programme as well as providing various necessities; these voluntary organizations at their height numbered as many as 140. Inside Kampuchea, in Phnom Penh, at best 30 international governmental and non-governmental aid organizations have carried out their activities. The overwhelming majority of relief organizations that

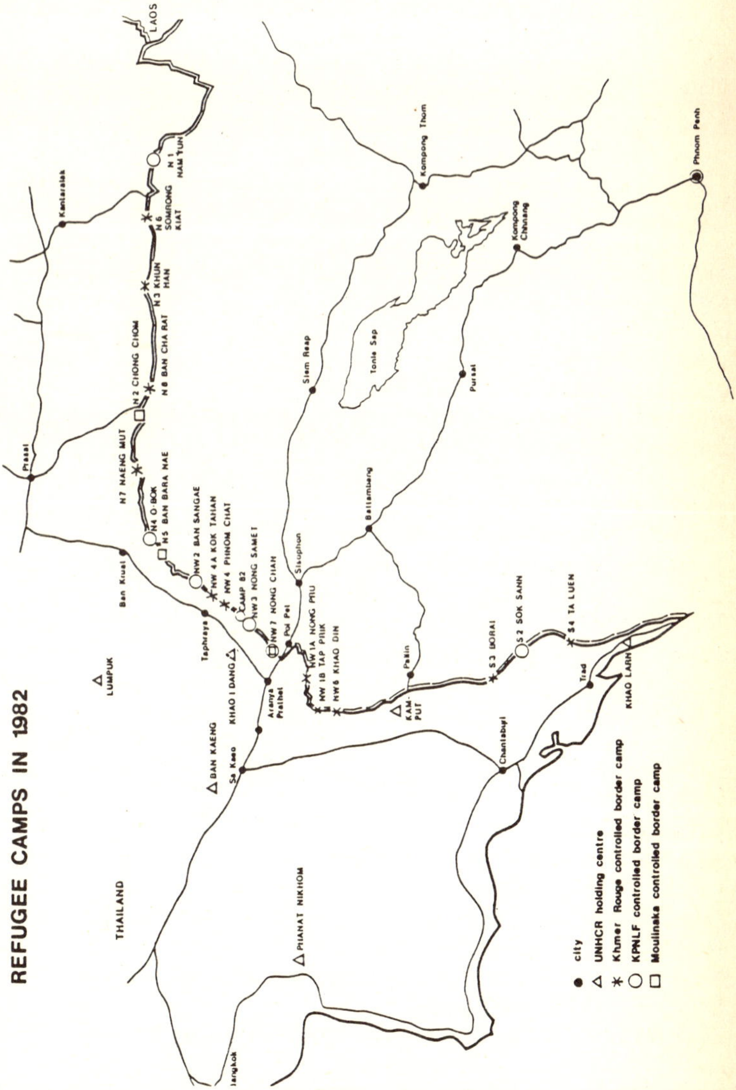
REFUGEE CAMPS IN 1982
THAILAND
LAOS
N 1 NAM YUN
N 6 SOMRONG KIAT
N 3 KHUN HAN
N 8 BAN CHA RAT
N 2 CHONG CHOM
N 7 NAENG MUT
N4 O-BOK
N5 BAN BARA NAE
NW 2 BAN SANGAE
NW 4A KOK TAHAN
NW 4 PHNOM CHAT
CAMP 82
NW 3 NONG SAMET
NW 7 NONG CHAN
NW 1A NONG PRUU
NW 1B TAP PRIK
NW 6 KHAO DIN
S 3 BORAI
S 2 SOK SANN
S 4 TA LUEN
KAM-PUT
KHAO LARN
KHAO I DANG
BAN KAENG
LUMPUK
PHANAT NIKHOM
Kantaralak
Prasat
Ban Kruat
Taphraya
Aranya Prathet
Sa Kaeo
Poi Pet
Sisophon
Siem Reap
Battambang
Pailin
Pursat
Tonle Sap
Kompong Thom
Kompong Chhnang
Phnom Penh
Chantaburi
Trad
Bangkok
city
UNHCR holding centre
Khmer Rouge controlled border camp
KPNLF controlled border camp
Moulinaka controlled border camp

have worked on the Thai side of the border have come from the United States. Most of these have earlier worked in Thailand and they have also had experience in Vietnam during the 1960s and at the beginning of the 1970s.[4]

Despite the relatively good material welfare, life in the refugee camps is coloured by insecurity. Life is led on the front lines and every border camp has its military units. Most of the border camps are only a few kilometres from the positions of Vietnamese and Kampuchean People's Republic troops. There are repeated clashes and occasionally shells have also hit civilian occupied sections of the camps.

The majority of the more than 300,000 refugees in the border area between Thailand and Kampuchea would be willing to leave the camps and move either to third countries or back home if a safe route through the lines were made possible. In 1979-80 a large number of refugees returned to Kampuchea (see Table 5), but during 1981 it became even more difficult to pass through the lines and the minefields that surround them and thus the total number of refugees has remained relatively stable. People have little by little accepted their fate of remaining more or less permanently rootless refugees. The freeze on the refugees situation feeds the continuation of the conflict in the area.

Large scale international relief activities have stabilized the refugee situation and given a crucial boost to the reorganization of the Kampuchean opposition movement. Similarly the Heng Samrin administration has been dependent on international relief programmes. One unavoidable side effect of efficient humanitarian relief activities is often the prolonging of a crisis. The reforming of the almost entirely destroyed Khmer Rouge system of control as well as the reinforcement of the military capacity of the various opposition movements has been made possible by international relief.

In principle, the aid provided by international organizations should go to only civilian refugees; in practice it is impossible for the organizations to supervise the final use of aid provided for refugees. In this context, relief provided for the border camps has proved especially problematic. The UN's World Food Programme has been responsible for the international acquisition of foodstuffs for relief activities and a separately established UN relief unit UNBRO (United Nations Border Relief Operation) has taken care of its distribution. During 1979-81 the distribution of food relief was handled by UNICEF and the International Red Cross. From the beginning of 1982 distribution was taken over by the newly established special unit, UNBRO.

Regularly distributed consignments of food are provided to the women and children living in the camps according to the number of individuals. After that the organizations are not able to supervise where the relief goes. The men in the camps are soldiers and naturally they also consume some of the food. In addition, international relief to the camps in the northern and southern border zones, which house about a third of the refugees and are 75% under Khmer Rouge control must be channelled through the Thai army (see Table 6). As for these shipments, the international relief organizations are not able to control to what degree or on what conditions the consignments are delivered. It is thought that the Thai government would not have originally permitted international relief to the Khmer refugees if it had not itself received part of the aid. On the basis of this demand a relief programme was started for Thai villagers in the border areas. Distribution in this programme is handled by a Thai army unit known as Task Force 80. It is also suspected that part of the international relief intended for camps in the northern and southern border zones has never reached its target recipients – it is suspected that the Thai army has taken about a quarter of the food aid it was meant to distribute to Khmer refugees.[5] Altogether it has been estimated that the percentage of loss in relief supplies directed to Khmer refugees through Thailand has risen to at least a third of the total.[6] Also, other emergency relief supplied mainly by voluntary organizations such as health services and essential goods for its part supports the military preparedness of the camps. For example a significant part of the medical services are used to treat wounded soldiers.[7]

The largest loss in relief aid was seen in the so-called land-bridge operation, in which food was distributed to peasants from the western parts of Kampuchea who came to the border. It was estimated that only a quarter of the aid reached the villages. The greatest part of this aid was used to pay for transport and middlemen, to ensure safety on the trip and in direct market sales. Many of these people were robbed and some soldiers living in the border camps posed as peasants who had come from inside Kampuchea. The land-bridge operation was discontinued in January 1981 because of its inefficiency. The government in Phnom Penh had taken a negative attitude towards the operation because the food relief – provided outside its scope of supervision, free of charge and which was in part used for speculation – had made more difficult the restarting of agricultural production in the western parts of the country and the implementation of its agricultural reforms.

Opposition Movements

The refugee camps in the border zones have formed support bases for opposition movements against the government of the People's Republic of Kampuchea. The chaotic flood of refugees in 1979 created the population basis from which the movements were able to draw their supporters. International aid in the form of food, medicine and weapons had made possible the organization of the movements. Thus the former centres for smuggling, the camps of criminal gangs and disorganized rightist guerrilla groups became gradually transformed into relatively well organized support areas for political-military opposition movements.

During 1979-80 there were often bloody power struggles for the control of the camps. 'Liberation movements' had been founded in the various camps and their leaders attempted to eliminate their political and military rivals. In addition to these Khmer Serei groups, the Khmer Rouge have also been able to retain control over part of the refugees which accompanied them: usually they isolated their own camps. Still as late as in 1980 there were, however, battles between the 'red' and 'white' Khmers for control of some of the camps. Since then relations between the opposition movements have stabilized despite mutual hostility and each has recognized the other's sphere of influence.

Militarily, the Khmer Rouge are still the most powerful opposition group. It is estimated that they have 30,000-40,000 soldiers under arms: they themselves claim a strength of 60,000 men plus another 50,000 soldiers in villages inside Kampuchea. The smallest estimate of their force is 20,000 soldiers, based on the Khmer Rouge's relatively poor military success.[8] In terms of civilian population, in any case, the power of the Khmer Rouge has sharply declined. The population of refugee camps under their control is a little over 100,000 (see Table 6). The largest camps are located in the border zone at the very edge of the border regions controlled by the Khmer Rouge. The new villages in these areas, the last vestiges of Democratic Kampuchea, are not self-sufficient, but rather rely on products brought in from Thailand; the currency in use, for example, is the Thai baaht. An estimated two-thirds of the demand for basic foodstuffs is satisfied by international relief. Medical services are received from international voluntary organizations; military aid is received from China or indirectly from the Thai army. In general, Democratic Kampuchea only exists by means of outside support.

The Kampucheans themselves for the most part angrily reject the Khmer Rouge who thus have obvious difficulty in maintaining their influence and in recruiting new soldiers. In order to break out of their isolation there has been an attempt to reform the public image of Democratic Kampuchea. The former Prime Minister and Party leader, Pol Pot, has stayed out of the public eye, and the more popular Khieu Samphan has received the Prime Minister's duties. The Communist Party has practised self-criticism and finally in 1982 dissolved itself: the Party's documents were ceremonially burned in public. A new judicial system has been created and Democratic Kampuchea has signed the UN Declaration of Human Rights. A new organization, the Patriotic and Democratic Front of Great National Union of Kampuchea (PDFGNUK), has been founded which has 'renounced the building of socialism and communism for tens or hundreds of years in order to mobilize a broad national front to crush the Vietnamese enemy, the Le Duan clique'.[9]

Democratic Kampuchea's liberalization programme has included encouragement of free enterprise: open markets are permitted in the refugee camps and people have the right to farm their own plots and marry at will. Even Buddhist monks have been invited into the Khmer Rouge areas. The changes are, however, to a large extent superficial: a Democratic Kampuchea government organization has replaced the Party machinery; former Party leaders have divided up the government duties: Pol Pot is the

Commander-in-Chief of the army, Ieng Sary is the Foreign Minister, Son Sen is the Minister of Defence, Ta Mok is the army Chief of Staff, etc.

Of the opposition movements only the Khmer Rouge have so far been able to carry out serious military strikes against the Vietnamese and the current Phnom Penh government. But even these, however, have been defensive measures and their future military position is weakening. They are not receiving the support of the population and support from the outside is indirect, with the exception of that received from China.

In future, a movement formed from the various Khmer Serei groupings may become the most important opposition power. There have been a dozen or so unco-ordinated Khmer Serei groups in the border region. The rightist organizations enjoy the more or less open political, material and military support of Thailand and the United States. Many international voluntary organizations work specifically in camps controlled by these groups. The recruitment of new members and soldiers from among the refugees is significantly easier for them than for the Khmer Rouge.

The largest and politically most important of the rightist movements is the KPNLF (Khmer People's National Liberation Front) which is led by a former Prime Minister of Sihanouk's time, Son Sann, and which has an army commanded by a former Lon Nol general, Dien Del. The KPLNF was founded in autumn 1979 with the combination of five anti-Pol Pot Khmer Serei groups. The movement has gradually gained control of various camps ruled over by smugglers and criminal gangs. By autumn 1980 the KPNLF had risen to the leading position in the rightist movement, but not until after a bloody power struggle among the different Khmer Serei factions. In spring 1982 its strength was estimated at some 5,000-9,000 soldiers. Dien Del himself claims his troop strength to be 12,000 soldiers plus another 10,000 soldiers inside Kampuchea.[10] The KPNLF controls some of the largest refugee camps, the most important of which are the Nog Samet and Nong Chan camps and the Sok Sann camp in the south. At the moment the movement controls approximately 100,000 refugees (see Table 6) and with the help of the Thai army it takes over most of the refugees which come from or are transferred from UNHCR holding centres to the border.[11] Among smugglers KPNLF agents and soldiers have infiltrated into Kampuchea, but they have not begun widespread fighting except in the southern zone. Military training is, however, well established and the movement has received growing amounts of military aid from the Thai army.

Another rightist opposition movement worth consideration is comprised of diverse forces grouped behind the former head of state, Prince Sihanouk. Prince Sihanouk still has appeal and support because of his royal background, especially among the older rural population. This has made it possible for him to play a central role in diplomatic attempts to create a coalition government. Sihanouk, however, lacks a strong political and military movement on which to rely. In spring 1981 a party was founded in Pyongyang, North Korea, under the name of the National United Front for an Independent, Neutral, Peaceful and Co-operative Cambodia (FUNCINPEC), but it is mainly just a facade created for international negotiations. It has great difficulties in attaining broad organizing support because of the extent to which it is tied to Sihanouk's shifting policy.

Some small mutual competing Khmer Serei groups which operate in the border zone have, however, given their support to Sihanouk's diplomatic efforts. They have fallen in behind the Moulinaka military organization (Mouvement pour la Liberation National du Kampuchea) founded by Kong Sileah in 1979.[12] At first Sihanouk rejected this support, but changed his attitude once he again began to aspire to a position of more active political power. The Moulinaka, however, has control of only two small refugee camps in the northern border zone and part of the Nong Chan camp, housing altogether just over 10,000 refugees (see Table 6).[13] The Sihanoukists were late in their organization work among the refugees and received only very guarded support from Thailand and the United States. China has provided enough aid to arm 3,000 soldiers, but in the spring of 1982 the strength of the Moulinaka's armed forces was only an estimated 700-1,500 men. They themselves claim their troop strength to be 5,000 soldiers.[14]

All of the opposition movements operating among the Khmer refugees are relatively weak, lack organized support inside Kampuchea and their activities are largely dependent on international support. Thailand and the United States supply the KPNLF, China supports the Khmer Rouge and Prince Sihanouk's Moulinaka movement receives political support from some non-aligned nations and military aid from China. None of the groupings alone, however, forms a credible political or military alternative to the present Phnom Penh government. Finally, in the summer of 1982, because of pressure from outside forces, mainly the ASEAN countries, United States and China, a coalition government was successfully formed including all three groupings.

Its President is Prince Sihanouk, the Prime Minister is Son Sann and the Deputy Prime Minister is Khieu Samphan. The government takes decisions on the basis of consensus and all the parties are represented in each of the most important ministries. The institutions of Democratic Kampuchea are used as the organizational basis of the coalition's administration up to and including the name, even though both Sihanouk and Son Sann had previously refused to act in the name of Democratic Kampuchea.[15]

These groupings, however, have such different backgrounds and are so hostile to one another that it is very difficult to construct a lasting alliance merely on the basis of their joint opposition to the Vietnamese. Only the gradual strengthening in the position of the Phnom Penh government along with the help of international pressure has forced them into co-operation. In fact the attempt at forming a coalition demonstrates the political and military weakness of the resistance movement. The forces that are now undertaking joint co-operation have often been each other's main opponents during different periods over the past 20 years. At the end of the 1960s it would not have seemed credible that just over 10 years later Prince Sihanouk would be simultaneously allied with both the Khmer Rouge against whom he fought a civil war and the Khmer Serei which overthrew him in the Lon Nol coup accusing him of being too soft against the Khmer Rouge.

The central motive for the formation of the loose coalition government has been to ensure that Kampuchea's representation in the UN remains with Democratic Kampuchea which has otherwise suffered a gradual loss of credibility in the international community. Negotiations carried out concerning the coalition government have been coloured by the lack of trust among the various parties, a fact which has emphasized the unreality of the talks. They have not divided real power within Kampuchea, but rather have concentrated on arguing over diplomatic representation in international forums.

Notes

1. Under a proposal by the government of Thailand all UNHCR centres would be closed by the end of 1982 except for the Khao I Dang and Phanat Nikhon receiving centres for transfer to third countries. During 1981 the Mairut and Kab Chreng holding centres were already closed.
2. According to a statement given to the Kampuchea Inquiry Commission by the Secretary General of Thailand's national security council, Prasong Soonsiri, the aim of Thailand's refugee policy is to transfer all the refugees in UNHCR holding centres back to their homeland. It is the refugee's own affair if they remain in camps along the frontier rather than returning to Kampuchea. According to him it would be desirable at this stage, as long as the military situation continues in Kampuchea, for a safety zone to be formed between Thailand and Kampuchea which would possibly be maintained by international relief organizations.
3. Statement by UNHCR South-east Asia representative Alan J.F. Simmance to the Kampuchea Inquiry Commission.
4 See for example Frances L. Starner, mimeo, Bangkok, 1980, and 'Who Grew Fat on Kampuchea Operation?', *Asiaweek*, 27 February 1981.
5. Ibid., and John McBeth, 'A Quiet Security Role', *Far Eastern Economic Review*, 23 January 1981; John Pilger claims that Task Force 80 has also led some Khmer guerrilla units in attacks into Kampuchea. Task Force 80 receives a significant part of its financing from the United States through the Embassy in Bangkok; John Pilger, 'America's Second War in Indochina', *New Statesman*, 1 August 1980.
6. Estimates given to the Kampuchea Inquiry Commission by the WFP's Bangkok office and the UNBRO's Aranyaprathet office concerning the outcome of food relief activities.
7. A Finnish medical team working in the surgical section of the Khao I Dang holding centre hospital in 1982 told the Kampuchea Inquiry Commission that 80-85% of the section's cases were operations connected with mine injuries or wounds caused by shooting and shrapnel; there were some 10 such cases per day. Each of the border camps has its own health care centre from which the seriously injured are taken to the hospital at Khao I Dang. Its level of care is better than in local Thai hospitals and the Khmers generally do not wish to

be treated in Thai hospitals because of discrimination.

8. Statement to the Kampuchean Inquiry Commission by Democratic Kampuchean representative Bun Kim. Compare Sven Öste, 'Kampuchea bricket in krigsspel' (Kampuchea a pawn in a game of war), *Dagens Nyheter*, 20 March 1982.
9. Communiqué by the Central Committee of the Communist Party of Kampuchea Concerning the Dissolution of the Communist Party of Kampuchea, Democratic Kampuchea, 6 December 1981.
10. Statement to the Kampuchea Inquiry Commission to General Dien Del. Dien Del was said to have resigned as chief of staff of the KPNLF in November 1982, after the killing of a KPNLF regimental commander. *Far Eastern Economic Review*, 5 November 1982.
11. KPNLF representatives are permitted by the Thai army to enter UNHCR holding centres to carry out political recruitment. This is in contradiction of UNHCR principles, but the organization has been powerless to control the situation.
12. Kong Sileah died in the summer of 1981 and the Sihanoukists accused the KPNLF of poisoning him. There has not, however, been any convincing evidence of this even though the KPNLF is attempting to policitally and militarily eliminate the Moulinaka. Another former Khmer Serei chief, In Tam, followed Kong Sileah as military commander.
13. The Moulinaka unit commander at the Nong Chan camp is a former Lon Nol army colonel, Nhem Sophon. The Khmer Serei group supporting Sihanouk in the O'Ksach camp is commanded by Tuon Chay and the commander at the O'Smach camp is a former Lon Nol general, Tiep Ben, who returned from the United States.
14. Estimate given to the Kampuchea Inquiry Commission by the Moulinaka commander of Nong Chan camp, Nhem Sophon.
15. John McBeth, 'None for All and All for None', *Far Eastern Economic Review*, 16 July 1982 and Jacques Bekaert, 'Kampuchea's "Loose Coalition": A Shotgun Wedding', *Indochina Issues*, No.22, December 1981.

5. The Interests of Power Politics

The problems of Kampuchea during the 1970s were centrally tied to the development of the whole of the region of Indo-China and its position in the international order. Indo-China is for its part a section of South-east Asia which in addition to the Indian subcontinent is one of the few parts of the world where the alleged security interests and spheres of influence of each of the three great powers are fundamentally opposed to one another. It is thus in both strategic location and significance very important, being a very inflammable area in the whole global great power setting.[1]

During the war in the Pacific (1941-5) Japan occupied the colonies of the Western nations in South-east Asia. Despite Japan's defeat in the Second World War the colonial powers were no longer able to permanently reinstate their rule in the former colonies. France became involved in drawn-out conflicts and the first Indo-China war (1946-54) ended only after the signing of the Geneva Peace Treaty in 1954. The Americans replaced the French in order to defend the 'free world' in accordance with the Truman Doctrine against what was seen as expansionism by China and the Soviet Union. Thus arose the second Indo-China war (1960-75). For ideological reasons the United States attempted to suppress Vietnam's nationalist movement. This, however, led to violations of the sovereignty of Vietnam's neighbouring countries, and to a war. Not until the Paris peace talks of 1973 was agreement reached on the withdrawal of the Americans. In May 1975 the government of South Vietnam lead by Thieu was finally overthrown making possible the reunification of Vietnam the next year. A few weeks earlier in Kampuchea, the Khmer Rouge had conquered the capital, Phnom Penh. Meanwhile in Laos during the summer of 1975 the Pathet Lao liberation movement strengthened its position within the two-year-old coalition government and in December it declared the establishment of the People's Democratic Republic of Laos under its own leadership. The second Indo-China war had come to an end and it was believed that the fighting which had continued almost uninterrupted since the Second World War had finally ceased.

But a lasting peace had not even yet been achieved in the region. The latter part of the1970s witnessed the outbreak of a new type of hostilities in Indo-China. Former allies found themselves on different sides of the lines.

Vietnam was at war with both Kampuchea and China while Laos had had border clashes with China. And this third Indo-China war continues.

The Third Indo-China War

There have been repeated engagements between China and Vietnam in the South China Sea. The dispute is over ownership of strategically and economically important islands in the area. China also has strong military forces on its border with Vietnam, while similarly Vietnam has increased the strength of its army within a few years from 600,000 to one million soldiers. China has concentrated troops also on its border with Laos, as a result of which Laos put an end to all Chinese aid activities in spring 1979. There are 40,000 Vietnamese soldiers in Laos and it is to be feared that border violations on the frontier with China could explode into a large scale military conflict. There are 180,000 Vietnamese soldiers in Kampuchea who are engaged in fighting guerrillas operating along the border with Thailand. There have also been clashes between the regular armies of Thailand and Vietnam.

The conflict between Vietnam and Democratic Kampuchea, which finally led to the entering of Vietnamese troops in 1979 and which brought the third Indo-China war to general notice, arose from the combined effect of a number of different factors. Its primary background is to be found in historical prejudices and the traditional contrasts between different nations. Secondly, the ideological and tactical disagreements among the Communist Parties which had led the liberation movements brought about mistrust among the new governments after the revolution. Thirdly, there have traditionally been disputes between Vietnam and Kampuchea over the frontier drawn by the French and the material and strategic advantages connected with the land and sea areas in question as well as over ownership of natural resources, regardless of what kind of government has been in power in Phnom Penh or Saigon.

The traditionally hard feelings between these nations, the border disputes and the arguments between their Communist Parties would have hardly, however, been sufficient reason for finally falling into broad scale military action. Not until disputes among the great powers were reflected in the region did relations worsen crucially between Vietnam and Kampuchea.[2] The setting for the basic confrontation of the third Indo-China war arose primarily from the gradual weakening in relations between China and Vietnam which in turn have been affected by the polarization in great power relations and the strategic changes which took place in these relations during the latter half of the 1970s.

The contradictions between Vietnam and China are the result of historical, regional, power-political and ideological factors which are just as complicated as those contributing to the conflict between Vietnam and Kampuchea.[3] The national confrontations rooted in history and dictated by geopolitical position have been independent of the social changes which have occurred in these countries. Both countries have a legitimate security need, the primary nature of which has been determined by sheer geography. On its western border Vietnam is extremely vulnerable, so relations with its two smaller neighbours are of strategic significance for its security. Similarly, for China Indo-China has for centuries formed a stepping stone which foreign powers have tried to use in order to invade China itself. In fact Chinese strategy during the whole of the second Indo-China war was based on calculations according to which the resistance by the Vietnamese functioned as a shield preventing the United States from attacking China itself.

The United States for its part based its participation in the Indo-China war on defeating what it saw as attempts at hegemony in the region by China and the Soviet Union. The liberation movements of Indo-China were supported in their war against the Americans by both of the socialist great powers, but these relations were neither uncomplicated nor without tensions. Differences in stress and conflicts of interest did not, however, become obvious until after the war. Neither Vietnam nor Kampuchea had fought the war in order to become immediately tied to some third great power. Kampuchea under the leadership of the Khmer Rouge attempted to completely isolate itself from the outside world, while Vietnam tried to build as extensive as possible a network of foreign contacts in order to avoid one-sided relations of dependence. For example it joined international financial institutions led by the Western nations such as the World Bank (IBRD), the International Monetary Fund (IMF), and the Asian Development Bank (ADB) and was prepared to accept direct foreign investment in addition to economic aid from the West.

The setting changed, however, as internal confrontations in the region of Indo-China sharpened. Khmer Rouge-led Kampuchea had not sought nor received recognition from the Soviet Union and in its antagonism towards Vietnam it sought support from China. The increasing tensions between the socialist great powers, China and the Soviet Union, had become problematic for Vietnam already during the second war. It had skilfully striven to maintain a balance in order to maximize support from both directions. Gradually, however, Vietnam came to rely to an increasing extent on the Soviet Union not least of all because in that direction there were none of the kind of historical and geopolitical strains which existed with China. The increasingly clear *rapprochement* by the latter with the United States, however, proved crucial. Beginning in 1972 when China defined the Soviet Union as its main opponent and began building closer relations with its enemies, Vietnam became even more estranged from the goals of its neighbour's foreign policy. China in turn began to experience ever greater mistrust towards Vietnam, fearing its possible alliance with the Soviet Union. Quite foreseeably, the unification of Vietnam in 1975, the birth of the world's third largest socialist country and the formation of the strongest of all the nations bordering on China's Asian frontier was considered as a potential security policy risk in Peking. Already during the same year China offered Vietnam a joint security treaty which contained a condemnation of all 'attemps at regional hegemony' – an indirect reference to the Soviet Union – but Vietnam rejected the proposal. On the other hand, Democratic Kampuchea was prepared to sign a communiqué with similar contents and thus gain support from China in its antagonism towards Vietnam.[4] The deepening confrontations in Indo-China offered the Soviet Union opportunities to expand its ties and influence in Vietnam. The structures of new alliances began to take shape.

United States strategy in South-east Asia following the defeat in the Indo-China war has been constructed on four elements: a) the discrediting of the new governments in Indo-China; b) the prevention of structural changes in other South-east Asian countries; c) the isolation and destabilization of Vietnam; and d) the deepening of contradictions among the socialist countries especially by the one-sided development of relations with China. The United States has been able to expand its regional influence through the realization of these goals much more successfully than it was able to in the second Indo-China war with a power policy based on armed might.

The events of the 1970s in Indo-China – wars among the socialist countries, the problem of the 'boat people' refugees, the exceptionally violent revolutionary government of the Khmer Rouge – offered the Americans an opportunity to re-evaluate the bases of their war in Indo-China. By increasing current tensions in the area the United States is able to make its earlier military actions seem as if they were justified. This then for its part supports attempts to legitimize a possible new, more active US policy in the Third World.

It was in the interests of the United States to drive a wedge between China and Vietnam at the first sign of a crack in their bilateral relations. Already during the second Indo-China war President Nixon and Secretary of State Kissinger exploited the dispute between the Soviet Union and China in order to weaken resistance by the Vietnamese. Since the end of the war the Americans have not wanted to establish diplomatic and economic relations with Vietnam, nor to provide aid as laid out in the peace agreement. On the contrary, the country has had trade sanctions imposed on it and there has been an attempt to isolate it from outside relations.

At the same time as US relations with Vietnam have become more distant, its relations with China have become closer. The matter is a question of global great power politics in which both the United States and China have a strategic interest in isolating the Soviet Union. As the situation has become more tense the room for manoeuvre by countries striving for non-alignment has become less – especially for those countries located in the immediate vicinity of the great powers or within their spheres of influence. As a neighbour of China, Vietnam as well was faced with a choice in its security policy.

In 1978 the new relations of alliance within the power politics setting of

South-east Asia were sealed, a fact which has had a basic reflection also in the global great power balance. The United States and China established diplomatic relations and have gradually expanded their joint co-operation. In the same year China and Japan signed a treaty on friendship and co-operation in which there is an indirect reference to checking the growth of the Soviet Union's influence in the Far East. At the same time it implicitly expresses support for a US military presence in the region. The Chinese leadership has also given support for the armament of Japan and Japan's security treaty with the United States.[5]

As a counterbalance, the nations of Indo-China have gradually come closer to the Soviet Union. As the room for manoeuvre in Vietnam's security policy lessened, as its external relations became more restricted and as its dispute with China deepened, the country came to rely on the Soviet Union to an ever increasing extent. In the summer of 1978 Vietnam became a full member of Comecon (CMEA) and a little later signed an agreement on friendship and mutual assistance with the Soviet Union,[6] thus gaining for itself both economic aid and security guarantees. At the same time, however, the Vietnamese government rejected a plan for the stationing of Soviet missiles and naval bases in the country. Despite this, these foreign policy moves were seen by China as extremely hostile acts.

Tension increased between these two countries to the point of war: Vietnam expelled its Chinese minority and in turn China closed its neighbour's consulates and ended all aid to it in the spring of 1978. A half a year after the break in relations, Vietnam secured its rear in Kampuchea. After gaining guarantees of non-interference from the United States, China attacked Vietnam in February 1979. In a military operation lasting less than a month a force of 320,000 Chinese troops attempted to completely destroy the 30 km-deep area occupied in northern Vietnam in order to 'teach a lesson' to its neighbour. This was intended as a demonstration of the bitterness felt over Vietnam's indifference to China's security interests and to demonstrate the limited nature of the security guarantees given by the Soviet Union.[7] China accuses Vietnam of drifting into the Soviet Union's sphere of influence, but Vietnam has actually turned to the Soviet Union to a greater extent only the more isolated it feels itself to be and the greater it sees the threat of China. Stopping the attack by China has been considered a great feat of defence in Vietnam. The aim of the attack was not, however, at any time intended to progress any deeper into Vietnam, a fact demonstrated for example by the absence of air support. A more important military goal was to tie down as much of the manpower of the Vietnamese army as possible and thus indirectly provide support for the Khmer Rouge in Kampuchea where the military situation had not yet come to a conclusion.

Instead of 'teaching a lesson', however, the use of direct military force has further polarized the internal contradictions within Indo-China and has dangerously increased tensions in great power relations as well. An end to Indo-China's third war seems more remote than ever, especially as it receives ever more impulses also from outside interests. The potentital for even wide-scale armed conflict in Indo-China dangerously exists. China's strategic *rapprochement* with the United States is perhaps the most significant move since the Second World War in terms of the global great power balance. In South-east Asia, and especially in Indo-China, the soundness of this new combination has been most importantly put to a test. Thus in being closely connected with the East-West confrontation in power politics the internal problems of Indo-China may pose a threat to world peace.

Diplomatic Efforts

Vietnam's involvement in Kampuchea has given full reinforcement to the earlier-formed structure of the power policy combinations in South-east Asia. The crisis in Kampuchea has intensified the strategic rapprochement between China and the United States. It has also offered China the opportunity to draw closer to the ASEAN countries. The goal has been to isolate Vietnam and in this way reduce its influence and that of the Soviet Union in Asia. Under the leadership of the United States, trade sanctions have been declared against Vietnam and all western aid and development co-operation activities (with the exception of the Nordic countries) have been blocked. There is a desire to punish Vietnam for sending its troops into Kampuchea and for drawing too close to the Soviet Union. But, as a result of just this policy of isolation, Vietnam has come to rely economically, politically and militarily even more greatly on the socialist nations of Europe. This in turn has increased the Soviet military presence in the area where previously it had no foothold.[8]

At the initiative of the ASEAN countries, the Kampuchean question has been discussed in the UN: the aim has not been, however, to find a realistic solution to the problem, but rather to create the widest possible front for the condemnation of Vietnam. This has also succeeded in that in practice only the socialist countries have opposed resolutions by the UN General Assembly demanding the total and immediate withdrawal of foreign troops from Kampuchea and respect for the country's right of self-determination. The vast majority of the member nations, including most of the non-aligned countries, have joined in supporting these resolutions. In a UN General Assembly vote in 1982 on a resolution concerning the situation in Kampuchea, the division was 100 in favour, 25 opposed and 19 abstentions, the latter group including Finland, Mexico and India. Finland was the only Western nation which abstained, basing its voting behaviour on its aim of avoiding stands on issues concerning a conflict of interests between the great powers. For Vietnam it has undoubtedly been especially annoying to become diplomatically isolated, particularly within the movement of non-aligned nations.

Only socialist countries, and of the most significant non-aligned nations only India, have recognized the People's Republic of Kampuchea and established diplomatic relations with the government of Heng Samrin.

Thus the majority of UN members continue to uphold the right of Democratic Kampuchea to represent the country in the world organization. However, year after year the number of nations voting for acceptance of Democratic Kampuchea's credentials has gradually decreased. India proposed in 1979 that Kampuchea's UN seat be left empty because of the unclear situation, but this has been viewed as a partial concession to the Heng Samrin government which could later more easily demand the place for itself. Instead, efforts were under way, led by the ASEAN countries, to form a coalition government comprised of the Khmer Rouge and the rightist resistance movements which could represent Democratic Kampuchea and thus improve its credibility within the world organization. Prince Sihanouk did in fact speak as the representative of the coalition government in the UN General Assembly in 1982. This helped increase support for Democratic Kampuchea in the vote on its credentials. Vietnam, for its part, has announced that as long as Democratic Kampuchea is represented in the UN, the world organization has no possibilities of contributing to a solution to the Kampuchean question.

The impotence of the UN to find a solution to the Kampuchea dispute has also been seen in the work of the Security Council. It has functioned merely as a forum for discussion in efforts to settle the situation in Southeast Asia, not having achieved even a single resolution on the matter. In the summer of 1981 an international Kampuchea conference was held which was organized on the basis of a UN General Assembly approved resolution made at the initiative of the ASEAN countries.[9] It was clear from the start that regardless of what kind of model for a solution the conference were to offer it would not have the concrete prerequisites for implementation. Vietnam and the Soviet Union along with its allies considered the conference to be biased and illegal and they did not participate in its work. Thus the conference lacked the prerequisites for success and its purpose was not to find a solution to the real problem. The conference was used to induce pressure and to isolate Vietnam and its allies within the international community and thus it only demonstrated and further sharpened the confrontation between the parties to the Kampuchea dispute. A side effect of the conference was a reinforcement of Democratic Kampuchea's status as the representative of the country.

The declaration approved unanimously by the conference demanded the immediate and complete withdrawal of Vietnamese troops from Kampuchea, respect for the country's right of self-determination and UN supervised elections for choosing a new government. Despite formal unanimity there were in the background of the conference strong differences between the most active participants, the ASEAN countries and China. The United States, in accordance with its tougher foreign policy and in an attempt to strengthen its China relations, was more inclined to side with the stand of the Chinese than with the ASEAN countries. Of the latter, especially Indonesia and Malaysia have been inclined to understand Vietnam's views and to recognize its legitimate security interests as regards Kampuchea. In the strategic reckonings of Indonesia and Malaysia above all China is seen as a threat factor in the long term – not least of all because of the powerful Chinese minorities in these countries – and a strong Vietnam is believed to be a counterbalance in this power policy setting. Furthermore, Indonesia and Malaysia have stressed that the inflamed Kampuchean situation has strengthened not only China's influence in the area, but also that of the Soviet Union.

Of the ASEAN counties Thailand has been the least desiring of compromise. For the more cynical of Thai calculations the maintenance of a crisis situation in neighbouring Kampuchea has been advantageous. In the first place it increases the political and military weight of Thailand in the strategic reckoning of the West and gives the country an opportunity to pressure the United States to increase military aid.[10] As for controlling Thailand's internal conflicts, the Kampuchean crisis has been of benefit in that guerrilla activities by the Communist Party in northern parts of the country have died down mainly because of reduced support from China; the number of guerrillas is estimated to have significantly declined after 1979. These factors explain why the government of Thailand has been unwilling to bring under control the export of arms to the opposition movements in Kampuchea and covertly has been ready to provide support areas, to build strategic road connections in the direction of the border and to create buffer zones in the border areas occupied by refugees and controlled by opposition movements, not to speak of possible direct military participation in operations against the Vietnamese.

In addition to China, the United States has sharply increased support for both the Kampuchean resistance movements and for armed opposition groups operating in Laos and Vietnam.[11] These movements have no possibility of militarily crushing Vietnam, but their actions can deepen the country's internal economic and social difficulties which would further isolate it and its allies within the international community. This is also the aim of the military tension maintained by China on Vietnam's northern border.

The continuation of the refugee problem in Indo-China has created instability and the need for a great power presence in the region. The United States has sharply increased its humanitarian aid to Khmer refugees via Thailand. Prosperous camps, which are advertised in, for example, Voice of America broadcasts directed to Kampuchea, are meant to attract more refugees and thus weaken the prestige of the current Phnom Penh government. Similarly, widespread but poorly documented claims of the use of chemical weapons in the region of Indo-China are primarily related to the structure of the confrontation in great power politics.[12]

For Vietnam, on the other hand, a real 'Kampuchean problem' does not even exist. The problem is only 'China's attempts at hegemony' in South east Asia. Thus negotiations for calming the situation should take place on three different levels and in three different phases. Firstly, talks should be carried out on pacifying the border between Thailand and Kampuchea;

secondly, negotiations should be held between the countries of Indo-China and the ASEAN countries on the general situation in South-east Asia; and thirdly, there should be negotiations with China on a non-aggression pact and on pacifying their joint border.

The other side, for its part, takes the view that the inclusion of the People's Republic of Kampuchea in the negotiations would mean its tacit recognition. Furthermore, a three-phase strategy of negotiations would on the one hand lead to approval of the status quo established by the Vietnamese military action, and on the other hand it would make the other negotiating parties subject to Vietnam's alleged tactics of divide and rule. The problem to be solved would then no longer be Kampuchea's internal situation and international representation, but rather the settlement of the disputes among the various countries which have arisen from regional power politics. Furthermore, negotiations on only a limited regional basis do not seem realistic in that even Vietnam recognizes that the background is influenced by great power interests – for example from the direction of China as Vietnam claims. Most recently, Vietnam, along with the other nations of Indo-China has proposed an international conference also including the other countries of South-east Asia, the permanent members of the UN Security Council and India. The ASEAN countries, however, are adamant about keeping negotiations on the UN level.

The views of the parties seem to be fixed; no one is willing to make concessions in order to find a compromise solution. Vietnam is ready to improve relations with the other nations of South-east Asia and with China on the condition that they approve the status quo which has been created under Vietnam's leadership. The ASEAN countries for their part require the complete withdrawal of Vietnamese troops from Kampuchea and UN supervised elections before they are prepared to recognize Vietnam's security needs and to undertake mutual contacts. On the other hand it is in the interests of China and the United States to polarize the situation and thus isolate Vietnam and its allies in the international community. The Kampuchean crisis has offered all of the great powers — including the Soviet Union — the opportunity for an active presence in South-east Asia.

The reckonings of power politics thus point to a continuation of the inflamed situation in Kampuchea. Vietnam will not withdraw its troops so long as the opposition movements receiving outside support operate from the border of Thailand. In fact as long as resistance by the Khmer Rouge continues, it legitimizes for the Kampucheans the presence of Vietnamese troops in the country. Thus, the stronger the resistance front is built up, the more permanent Vietnam's presence in Kampuchea will become. And in turn, the resistance will continue as long as the Vietnamese are in Kampuchea. This is a vicious circle that the Kampucheans do not have the ability to break out of and which the other parties do not have sufficient political will — and the need — to break.

Notes

1. See for example Michael Leifer, 'Conflict and Regional Order in Southeast Asia', *Adelphi Papers*, No.162, International Institute for Strategic Studies, London, 1980.
2. According to a statement given to the Kampuchea Inquiry Commission by Vietnam's Foreign Minister, Nguyen Co Thach, the presence of Vietnamese troops in Kampuchea has not been primarily based on humanitarian intervention, support for the Khmer rebels, expansionism by Vietnam, or self-defence against attacks by Democratic Kampuchea, but rather it is a matter of a precautionary measure to alleviate the threat posed by China in the region of Indo-China.
3. See for example Marek Thee, 'Red East in Conflict, The China/Indochina wars', *Journal of Peace Research*, Vol.XVI, No.2, 1979, and Dennis Duncanson, 'China's Vietnam war: new and old strategic imperatives', *The World Today*, June 1979; Elizabeth Becker, 'The Chinese Invasion of Vietnam: Changing Alliances', *Indochina Issues*, No.1, March 1979, and Lowell Finley, 'Raising the Stakes', *South East Asia Chronicle*, No. 64, September-October 1978, and Murray Hiebert, 'Vietnam's Ethnic Chinese', *Southeast Asia Chronicle*, No.68, December 1979.
4. Stephen R. Hèder, 'The Kampuchean-Vietnamese Conflict', *South-East Asian Affairs 1979*, Heinemann Educational Books Ltd, Singapore, 1979.
5. Chin Kin Wah, 'The Great Powers and Southeast Asia, A Year of Diplomatic Effervescence', *South-East Asian Affairs 1979*, Insitute of Southeast Asian Studies, Singapore, 1979, and Michael Yahuda, 'China's new outlook: the end of isolationism?', *The World Today*, May 1979.
6. The only military clause in the treaty of friendship and mutual assistance between Vietnam and the Soviet Union obliges both parties to undertake consultations on practical assistance measures if either of the parties to the treaty is attacked or threatened by attack. Thus the treaty does not include an automatic obligation for military co-operation as do the security agreements between the Soviet Union and the countries of Eastern Europe. In this respect it resembles more the agreements the Soviet Union has made with Finland and some Third World countries such as India.
7. Elizabeth Becker, op.cit., and 'The Power Game, Asia 1980 Yearbook', *Far East Economic Review*.
8. The Soviet Union has been desirous of gaining the right to permanent use of the former American air and naval bases at Cam Ranh Bay and Danang. Vietnam, however, has refused to approve of the establishment of Soviet bases on its territory. According to Vietnam's Foreign Minister this option is, however, being kept open in the event that Vietnam's security situation so requires. Statement by Nguyen Co Thach to the Kampuchea Inquiry Commission. The Secretary General of Thailand's security council, Prasong Soonsiri, has accused the Soviet Union of building naval bases on the coast of Kampuchea at Kompong Som and Ream, the latter of which was the site of a small naval station during the times of Sihanouk and Lon Nol, 'Prasong reveals Soviet naval build-up in Kampuchea', *Nation*, Bangkok, 10 March 1982. The activization of the Soviet Union's presence in Indo-China can be seen above all in fast growing economic co-operation and a massive

humanitarian aid programme. Also the Soviet Union's military aid to Vietnam and through Vietnam to Kampuchea is very significant.

9. International Conference on Kampuchea, 'Draft Report of the Conference', A/CONF.109/L.1/Add. 1, 17 August 1981.
10. Because of the tense situation in South-east Asia the United States is sharply increasing military aid to Thailand. In 1982 military aid rose by 25% to a record 67 million dollars. This is over twice as much as all other US economic aid to Thailand which in 1982 amounted to 27 million dollars in credits and grants. Thailand uses some 200 million dollars annually for arms purchases mainly from the United States.
11. In the summer of 1981, at the same time as the UN's International Conference on Kampuchea, there were meetings in New York and Washington which were attended by exiled opposition leaders from Indo-China who were attempting to organize opposition movements and arrange joint co-operation. Former leading rightist politicians and officers from Laos founded the ULNLF (United Lao National Liberation Front) and the VNSC (Vietnam National Salvation Committee) was founded for Vietnam. Traditionally the FULRO rebel movement (Front Uni pour la Lutte des Races Opprimees) has operated among the hill tribes of central Vietnam, and the Hmong hill tribes in southern parts of Laos have rebelled. Trusting in growing support from the Reagan administration these movements, along with the Khmer Rouge and the KPLNF, are attempting to undertake closer co-operation; Nayan Chanda, 'Fancy meeting you here', *Far Eastern Economic Review*, 24-30 July 1981. See also John Pilger, 'America's second war in Indochina', *New Statesman*, 1 August, 1980; Pilger sets out US political motives in its strong pressuring of the Kampuchean opposition movements.
12. On 22 March 1982 the US Department of State issued a report in which it renewed its claims that Vietnam, with the support of the Soviet Union, had used chemical weapons in Kampuchea. According to the report 981 people had been killed in this way in Kampuchea in recent years. According to the *New York Times*, the accusations are precise, but the evidence is not watertight; *New York Times*, 30 March 1982. According to the newspaper the only example consists of blood samples taken by an American medical officer, Col. Amos Townsend, from nine soldiers from the Khmer Rouge area, eight of which according to the US Department of Defense laboratory contained a mycotoxin known as T-2. The mould which produced this mycotoxin appears in tropical environments, although the specific T-2 mycotoxin has earlier been found only in arctic regions. The Foreign Minister of the People's Republic of Kampuchea in turn claimed to the Kampuchea Inquiry Commission that the United States had stationed chemical weapons in Thailand which were used against Kampuchea during the period of 11-14 February 1982, south of the Phnom Malai area, causing 20 civilian deaths. The Kampuchean Ministry for Foreign Affairs was either not willing or not able to provide more detailed evidence of the occurrence, and no interest was expressed in calling in an international investigation group.

    Similarly, the Kampuchea Inquiry Commission did not gather any evidence of the use of chemical weapons by Vietnam during a visit from the Thai side along the Kampuchean border in March 1982. Systematic inquiries on the matter were made among the international medical staffs of the border camps, but none had come across even suspected cases. In the same way a

UN inquiry delegation returned empty-handed from a visit to the area at the beginning of 1982. See Ted Morello, 'The jury stays out', *Far Eastern Economic Review*, 4 December 1981. Wide-scale use could not have been made of biochemical weapons without the knowledge of the medical staffs, and biochemical weapons are not used for individual cases. Not even Khmer Rouge troops, who according to claims have been the victims of chemical warfare since 1979, yet use gas masks.

The evidence gathered by the United States also seems flimsy. Why was Townsend in particular, a former US army doctor in South Vietnam, sent to gather the decisive blood samples? Convincing evidence will be gained when samples taken by a researcher with a neutral background are examined in a neutral laboratory. The seriousness of the accusations by the US government also seem out of proportion in view of the limited nature of the evidence.

In answer to a question by the Finnish Inquiry Commission whether there is evidence that specifically Vietnam has spread chemical poisons, Col. Townsend replied that probability indicates it. With just as great probability it could be said that some other country has used chemical weapons in Kampuchea if in fact they have been used at all. The alleged cases of poisoning have been found only in Khmer Rouge areas, not those controlled by other opposition movements. It could also be in the interest of some other countries – not Vietnam or its allies – to disseminate an easily identifiable mycotoxin in the area.

6. International Humanitarian Aid

Helena Tuomi, assisted by a working group

International recognition of the distress of the Kampuchean people in 1979 was slow. But once the issue started to attract more widespread attention, extensive humanitarian aid was set in motion both within Kampuchea and among Kampuchean refugees.

Developments in Kampuchea in the 1970s – from US bombings and the internal political struggle to the disasters of the Pol Pot period, the Vietnamese arrival, and new radical changes – more or less destroyed Kampuchean society and caused untold suffering to its people. Late as it was, the international community was left with one task: to try to save a nation in ruins.

The historical paradox of humanitarian work is that the need for it arises through open conflict of power interests – which then go on to hinder successful provision of humanitarian aid. Considering the immense humanitarian challenge facing the world in Kampuchea, one may thus well ask: was the political situation in the area such that this task could be successfully carried out?

Today, millions of people are in need of some form of humanitarian aid, many of them as a result of open military conflicts. The present analysis of the humanitarian programme for the people of Kampuchea, aims to deepen general understanding of the conditions under which humanitarian work is undertaken. The possible critical observations presented here can hopefully help strengthen the basis and improve the conditions for future humanitarian operations.

As far as the humanitarian programme in Kampuchea is concerned a full documentation of the interplay between humanitarian needs, aid operations and power politics is not possible: not all the necessary documents, e.g. those of the largest donors of humanitarian aid, are accessible. The findings presented here are therefore very preliminary. And thus the intention is not to give a final evaluation of the Kampuchean humanitarian programme, but only to participate in a discussion which aims at reinforcing conditions for humanitarian work in open political conflicts.

The Beginning of the Aid Programme

Uprootedness soon leads to a need for humanitarian aid. During the Vietnam war, about half the Kampuchean population was forced to flee to the cities. International humanitarian agencies provided emergency relief for these people, looked after the wounded and the sick, and visited prisoners of war.[1]

The Pol Pot period was characterized by forced relocations of people to the countryside, forced labour and a gradual destruction of all social and economic structures. International humanitarian agencies were not granted entry to Kampuchea. However, on some occasions the Khmer Rouge regime considered asking for international assistance; for instance malaria in Democratic Kampuchea was so serious that aid requests had to be considered.[2]

Although Democratic Kampuchea was isolated, some humanitarian organizations knew as early as 1978 that the situation in the country was serious. Having staff only in neighbouring countries, however, they had no access to detailed information.[3]

There was still little information at hand after the fall of the Khmer Rouge regime. But increasing attention was now being paid to the situation in Kampuchea, not only for political reasons, but also for humanitarian reasons. From January onwards, the International Committee of the Red Cross (ICRC) and UNICEF offered their help repeatedly through their contacts in Hanoi, but the offers were turned down: the officials suggested that aid be delivered to Hanoi from where it would then be sent on to Kampuchea for distribution. Humanitarian agencies are not, however, permitted to use third countries for aid delivery.

In February the US Embassy in Bangkok warned Washington that famine might break out in Kampuchea. For several months, the US administration neglected the warning, considering it too alarmist; not until August 1979 – after satellite photos had shown that only 10% of the rice-fields had been planted, and a month after the Heng Samrin government had appealed for food aid from the FAO – did the US State Department express its deep concern over growing evidence of famine. Yet nearly three months passed before President Carter announced on 24 October a pledge of US $ 69 million for famine relief in Kampuchea.[4]

Early in the spring, Thailand urged an international relief effort for Kampuchea, fearing that famine in the country would cause an influx of refugees into Thai territory.[5] Thailand did not want huge numbers of refugees in the country – only recently had she forced thousands of 'boat people' back to sea. As far as is known, no international relief was supplied at the Thai border in the spring.

In April and May, press reports began writing about a 'spectre of famine' in Kampuchea; this image was strengthened by the Kampuchean refugees making their way to the Thai border. In April 1979 some 200,000 Khmers fled Kampuchea into Thai territory; while 80,000 were allowed to cross the border the remainder were turned back. In early June 1979 the Thai Government again repatriated 40,000 Khmers to Kampuchea.[6] This would appear to be the period during which the Royal Thai Army started to place fleeing Khmer Rouge forces and other opposition groups in border encampments. Starting from June, Bangkok quietly allowed American food and medical supplies to cross the border into areas controlled by Khmer Rouge. The Thai military simply dropped food at the border, and civilians and soldiers alike came to pick it up, without any monitoring by relief organizations.[7]

It thus seems that a quiet bilateral relief effort had been started along the border before the international organizations were called in. The international relief effort started in June, when the Thai government invited UNICEF to visit the border and assess the needs of the Khmers in the border encampments. UNICEF earmarked US $ 200,000 for Khmer refugees in Thailand to be used by the Thai Ministry of Health for medical goods, materials for temporary shelter and emergency supplies. The World Food Programme (WFP) began providing rice for distribution by the Thai army along the border at the end of July 1979.[8]

But while the image of a 'spectre of famine' was spreading all around the world, authorities in Phnom Penh did not seem to be worried – at least they did not turn to the international aid agencies. With the data available at present, it is difficult to say what was behind this contradiction. The authorities were perhaps not fully aware of how serious the situation in the country actually was; or they may not have considered it serious at all; or they may have regarded the aid from Vietnam and other socialist countries as being sufficient.

Soon, however, attitudes started to change in Phnom Penh. In May and June the authorities in Hanoi wanted to discuss the situation in Kampuchea with the ICRC and UNICEF, but no agreements were reached. On 3 July the Heng Samrin regime asked the FAO in Rome for international food aid. Suprisingly, it now estimated that over two million people in Kampuchea were threatened by famine, and asked for 108,000 tons of rice plus vegetable oil and sugar

On 17 July 1979, the representatives of the ICRC and UNICEF arrived in Phnom Penh to study the needs for aid, but they were only allowed to stay for three days. What they saw was devastation, starvation, suffering and ruins; but again accurate information was not available for drawing up a detailed programme.

On 9 August ICRC and UNICEF representatives flew to Kampuchea with 4.4 tonnes of drugs and medical equipment; they also introduced their plans for assistance. The visit lasted a week and resulted in an agreement on relief flights between Bangkok and Phnom Penh. Permission was also given for an ICRC doctor and a UNICEF logistics specialist to enter Kampuchea, but no agreement was made on major emergency programmes.[9]

Negotiations continued: the Heng Samrin government wanted no aid to be given from Thailand to the border area, as this would only benefit the

Khmer Rouge; the aid organizations, on their part, emphasized that they must give aid to all who need it, without any discrimination. The Heng Samrin government evidently gave up on this question, since the joint ICRC/UNICEF emergency operation (later the Joint Mission) was finally launched on 13 October 1979.

The private voluntary organizations soon started coming in, too. The pioneers were a small French agency, La Comité Française d'Aide Medicale et Sanitaire à la Population Cambodgienne, and OXFAM. In partnership with 10 Catholic and Protestant relief organizations, their representatives flew their first aid flight of medical supplies to Phnom Penh on 24 August 1979. The representatives of these organizations, again, reported the destruction of the country, the malnutrition of the people and the lack of food, medical equipment – of everything.

In September OXFAM was instrumental in the formation of a consortium of over 30 non-governmental organizations for Kampuchean aid.[10] The NGO-Consortium agreed from the outset that no aid be given to the Khmer Rouge forces; all of their aid would go for civilians on strictly humanitarian grounds. The Phnom Penh government would take care of the distribution of aid, but the staff of the Consortium would be free to travel around and monitor the programme.

On 14-20 August the representatives of the World Council of Churches and the Christian Conference of Asia visited Kampuchea on a fact-finding mission. Following this visit, the WCC launched an appeal to the churches on 16 October 1979. The churches emphasized the need to satisfy the basic needs of ordinary people. Other notable aid donors were the CIDSE (International Co-operation for Socio-Economic Development), a consortium of Roman Catholic aid organizations from various countries, the ARRK which raised aid funds from the US Christian aid agencies (Action for Relief and Rehabilitation in Kampuchea), and World Vision International and, aid agency from California.[11]

Meanwhile, more refugees were gathering at the border of Thailand and Kampuchea, and the situation grew more serious. Aid agencies were negotiating future programmes with various parties, particularly with the Thai Government and Democratic Kampuchea. It seems that Pol Pot was originally opposed to international aid, but he reversed his position after Heng Samrin had appealed to the FAO. This was obviously to do with the battle between the two governments for international recognition,[12] although their real needs for aid naturally also forced them to look for all possible sources.

In mid-September the representatives of the ICRC and UNICEF crossed the border at Nong Pru and found about 60,000 people in a desperate plight. The Thai government reported that another 120,000 were pushing their way towards the border elsewhere. The first co-ordination meeting was now arranged on the ways and means of providing relief to the people of Kampuchea. The participants were the ICRC, the WFP and UNICEF, various Thai ministries and some Western embassies. On 26

September the ICRC and UNICEF submitted their plan for the delivery of assistance to the displaced persons in north-west Kampuchea. The operation would be a joint exercise of the ICRC and UNICEF, with security guaranteed by the Thai army. The ICRC, the WFP and UNICEF would deliver aid supplies to the Thai government warehouses; transport to the border would be taken care of by ICRC/UNICEF; transport across the border by the representatives of Democratic Kampuchea. The aid agencies would monitor the programme.

ICRC/UNICEF also reported their survey which showed that 60,000 people along the border were in a very difficult situation: 80% of the children were suffering from severe malnutrition, and malaria was rampant.[13]

The Thai government had made it clear from the very beginning that the aid agencies willing to use Bangkok as their base for deliveries to Kampuchea would have to give aid supplies to the border as well. On the other hand, the statutes of the humanitarian agencies – as well as the political pressures by the largest donors – were clear: victims of the political and military conflicts should be assisted both in areas controlled by Heng Samrin and Pol Pot forces. A totally different question was how this aid could be monitored on both sides and how the aid could be distributed between the various target groups.

The first emergency deliveries to the border encampments took place as follows: 5 October at Nong Pru, 11 October at Nong Samet, 14 October at Phnom Chat (at the request of the Thai army without an initial survey of the needs), 22 October at Tap Prik, the last week of October at Mak Mun, 3 November at Kok Sung, 16 November at Klong Kai Thuen. The deliveries were usually made after a survey of the needs. However, with people coming and going, it was impossible to keep any register of the populations in the border encampments.

On 16 December the aid agencies started a new form of operation: distribution of relief for Kampucheans who were not permanent residents in any encampments.[14] They came to the distribution depots at the border, picked up food or other essentials with them and went away. The history of this part of aid is unknown: the distribution for these non-residents came to be called the 'land-bridge', and it is this part of the operation that makes analysis of the border relief difficult. Non-residents were included in the aid agencies budgets and in the estimates of the size of the assisted population along the border, although they did not stay at the border.

On 17 October the Thai government announced that it would relax its strict border policy and allow displaced Kampucheans to enter Thai territory. A week later Thai soldiers began transportation of 31,000 sick and dying Khmers from the border to the first new centre, Sa Kaeo, 70 km from the border: there were as yet no facilities, pouring rain turned the whole area into a lake of mud – and suddenly thousands of dying, sick and starving people were brought in. Many experienced relief workers have said that it was the worst scene they had ever witnessed. This chaotic scene was to symbolize the whole Kampuchean relief programme for quite some time.

In October 1979 it was estimated that about 600,000 fleeing Khmers were gathering along the border, trying to cross into Thailand. Many observers feared that this would mean 20 new chaotic camps, comparable to Sa Kaeo, emerging in Thailand. If such an enormous influx took place within a short period of time, how would anyone be able to hand out relief in such chaotic circumstances?

As a continuation of its 'open door' policy, the Thai government asked the United Nations High Commissioner for Refugees (UNHCR) to assist in the construction of new centres for Kampucheans entering Thai territory. It asked the UNHCR to provide facilities for 300,000 Khmers and to assist in the care and maintenance of these people together with other relief agencies. The Thai proposal thus implied that half of the potential refugees be admitted to Thailand. The UNHCR drew up a US $ 60 million plan for the period 1 November 1979 - 30 June 1980, including the construction of six camps for new arrivals plus their basic care and maintenance. The UNHCR would supervise the camps, whereas the Thai Supreme Command would be responsible for administration. The ICRC, the WFP and private voluntary organizations would assist in the operation.[15]

The Thai military now started to transport people from the border to the new camps in Thailand. The Thai government did not recognize the Kampucheans in Thailand as 'refugees' in the international legal meaning, but called them 'illegal immigrants'. For this reason, the new camps were called 'holding centres' instead of 'refugee camps'. The Thai governments also considered these centres temporary – people should be resettled in third countries or return to Kampuchea as soon as possible.[16] However, being under UNHCR protection, *de facto* the Kampucheans who entered the centres supervised by the UNHCR were fairly safe: they could not, for example, be removed against their will. All residents in these centres were registered, and nobody could move in or out without permission.

Most of the people along the border wanted to get into the UNHCR camps. However, for most of them this proved impossible: the Thai immigration policy was very strict. The Thai government originally promised to take 300,000 immigrants from the border, but this turned out to be a gross exaggeration. Careful comparison of all available official and unofficial sources shows that there were 119,000 residents in the holding centres in December 1979, and their number reached a peak of 177,000 in May 1980 – after that, the figure has constantly decreased (93,500 in February 1982). Why the Thai authorities originally agreed on 300,000 people with the UNHCR and then permitted only half of them, is not known.

Those who tried to cross the border but were stopped by the Thai army had two alternatives: either they could move to the border encampments controlled by the armed units of the political groups, or they could return to Kampuchea. Those who opted for the border camps were stranded in the middle of a military area. The military units of Khmer Rouge, KPNLF or Moulinaka. These units were continuously fighting for control of these camps. In the north was the Thai army, in the south the Vietnamese forces. And as civilian and military areas were not clearly demarcated, the whole region was far from safe for civilians.

As far as Thailand was concerned, these people had no legal status – after all they were not in Thailand but in Democratic Kampuchea. Phnom Penh did not protect them, either, as it did not have military control over the area, nor any administration. For Phnom Penh, these people were guerrillas or their supporters. In the worst case, there could be three types of battles: those between the armed political units, those between the military units and Vietnamese forces, and those where the Vietnamese and the Thai forces were involved. The position of civilians could hardly have been worse. No wonder they often moved from one camp to another.

A further problem regarding civilians in the border camps was that while most of them may have entered the camps voluntarily, it is also possible that some of them were forced or persuaded. There are three reasons why the armed political groups may have needed civilians: 1) the political reason: the opposition groups needed to show that they control some groups and that these people support their political claims; 2) the economic reason: civilians were needed to make international humanitarian aid possible, and the civilians could help with the material supply of the armed units; and 3) the military reason: the presence of civilians would potentially protect the armed units against enemy attacks, i.e. civilians were used as a human shield. The third type of function is, although forbidden by the international legal rules on warfare, common in guerrilla activities. Finally, soldiers were recruited from the civilian population.

In sum, we may conclude that the creation of the border zone between Kampuchea and Thailand has been the most difficult part of the Kampuchean humanitarian problem. Those who created it bear a very heavy responsibility for the destiny of the civilians. From the humanitarian point of view it would have been logical to try to evacuate them from the area. If this was not politically possible, the second best solution would have been to try to clearly demarcate the civilian areas from the military ones and then give relief to the civilians until a more permanent solution could be found. Neither of these measures were undertaken, and humanitarian aid had to be started under very difficult circumstances.

After October 1979 it had become clear that the assistance programme for the Kampuchean people would have to include three distinct parts: the people in Kampuchea, the people in the border camps, and the people in the holding centres in Thailand. The creation of the border zone had also affected some Thai villages, the inhabitants of which were therefore in need of assistance, too, either because they were removed or suffered other material losses, or because their standard of living had to be brought to more or less the same level as that of the immigrating Kampucheans.

The international aid agencies, both governmental and voluntary, were all now ready to start a massive aid programme. They launched campaigns all now ready to start a massive aid programme. They launched campaigns to raise funds for the programme. The success of the campaigns is in the main attributable to the international mass media, which very efficiently put across the image of the Kampuchean nation facing the risk of extinction and the image of a dramatic refugee problem in Thailand.

On 19 October the ICRC/UNICEF mission launched their joint appeal, and a week later the Red Cross appealed to national Red Cross societies for medical personnel. On 5 November the first Donors meeting was held at UN headquarters in New York, chaired by Secretary-General Kurt Waldheim. The conference produced pledges of US $ 210 million in cash and kind for emergency assistance within Kampuchea, on the border and in Thailand: one of the largest humanitarian operations ever was under way.

In addition to international humanitarian aid, bilateral aid played a crucial role. In Kampuchea, this meant the aid supplied by Vietnam and the Soviet Union, as well as other socialist countries. In the case of Thailand, this meant her closest political allies.

Main Characteristics of the Aid Programme

The aid agencies had to decide how to cope with the tripartite structure of the operation. The OXFAM/NGO-Consortium chose to operate exclusively inside Kampuchea and not to deliver any aid to the border or to Thailand. OXFAM, as well as other voluntary organizations operating in Kampuchea, decided to use Singapore as their base because of political pressures in Thailand.

The ICRC/UNICEF Joint Mission, together with the WFP, had to distribute aid to all three areas due to their rules of neutrality – as well as because of the views expressed by the largest donors and Thailand. The Joint Mission used Thailand as its base of operations, which with Thailand and her allies as active parties to the conflict put it under more political pressures. Some voluntary organizations chose to operate exclusively in Thailand.

During the first few months it was difficult to give accurate estimates of the extent of the crisis and of how much aid would be needed. The estimates of the size of the Kampuchean population fluctuated between four and seven million, their priority needs being food aid, transportation and health care. As was mentioned earlier, the Phnom Penh authorities estimated in July that two million people faced the risk of starvation – but the aid agencies did not know where and how much aid would be needed.

Estimates of the extent of the 'refugee problem' were not very precise, either. It was probably generally expected that those 500,000-600,000 Khmers who had fled to the border would end up in Thai camps after Thailand's announcement of its 'open door' policy. The agencies thus expected a massive influx to the border and from there to Thailand in a very short time. The World Food Programme, for example, estimated that, from September on, it provided food for 300,000 people during the first two weeks, for 400,000 during the next three weeks, and for 620,000 people in November. At the beginning of December it sent a telegram to Rome requesting food aid for 750,000 people. The WFP reported that every day 7,500 more people were appearing at the border.[17]

It seems that the Thai government encouraged the view that it would allow a large influx to the Thai camps. According to a usually well-informed journal, the Thai government told the WFP that it would allow 5,000-10,000 new arrivals every day to the Kao I Dang camp in December. In the same camp the WFP was told that up to 20,000-50,000 new arrivals would be evacuated from the border every day because a Vietnamese attack at the border was to be expected.[18] Yet in December 1979 there were 119,000 residents in the camps maintained by the UNHCR; in January 1980 the number was up to 141,387. The aid agencies had prepared themselves for two or four times higher figures.

Where were the people, then? In the border encampments or drifting along the border? The estimates of the number of residents in the border camps have consistently been unreliable. The first figures were given by those who controlled the camps – the opposition groups – but the aid agencies complained that they inflated the figures to get more aid. The aid agencies tried to make their own surveys, but this was difficult. The official estimates have been 114,000 in March 1980; 160,000 in May 1980, 180,000 in June 1980; 116,000 in September 1980; 150,000 in March 1981.

The traffic to the border area and to the camps was controlled by the Thai army; there was no admittance to the camps in the northern and southern sectors. The central/north-western zone was supervised by the WFP and UNICEF, later by a special United Nations unit UNBRO (United Nations Border Relief Operation). In all camps internal control was in the hands of the Khmer political groups.

As we have seen, only a small percentage of refugees were able to go to Thailand, and many of them did not want to go to the dangerous border camps. The rest of those 600,000-800,000 Kampucheans who originally tried to emigrate were drifting around or returned to Kampuchea. Thus the whole refugee problem became entirely different to what had originally been expected.

So far it is impossible to say why relief was delivered to non-resident Kampucheans. Relief was given to them at the border, mostly at the entrance of some encampments. How was the need for aid estimated? As far as border relief goes, the aid agencies always included the non-residents, which makes the number of assisted people two or three times higher than the number of camp residents. In 1980-81 there were roughly as many residents in the Thai camps as in the border camps. By multiplying their combined number by two or three we get the total number that was usually quoted of all those who received international relief from Thailand.

and WFP gave most of the aid, whereas in the Thai camps the UNHCR bore the main responsibility, assisted by the ICRC.

We may conclude that, despite intimate co-operation, the division of labour between the agencies was different in all three areas of operation. Each aid agency had its special task and mandate, and they were also dependent on their decision-making bodies when choosing how to operate in different conditions.

Table 8
Shares of Aid Agencies in Three Aid Areas
October 1979-January 1981 (millions of US $ and percentages)

Area	*ICRC*	*UNICEF*	*WFP*	*FAO*	*UNHCR*	*Total*
Kampuchea						
$	34.3	68.7	105.3	44.5	3.9	256.7
per cent	13	27	41	17	2	100
Border						
$	45.5	13.7	44.0	—	—	103.2
per cent	44	13	43	—	—	100
Holding centres						
$	18.7	—	—	—	95.8	114.3
per cent	16	—	—	—	84	100
Affected Thais						
$	1.3	1.2	12.5	—	—	15.0
per cent	9	8	83	—	—	100
Total $	*99.8*	*83.6*	*162.3*	*44.5*	*99.7*	*489.2*
Per cent	*21*	*17*	*33*	*9*	*20*	*100*

In an operation with conflicting political parties, it is always necessary to pay attention to the distribution of aid between different parts of the aid programme. As Table 9 shows, the organizations' aid policies differed to some extent from each other.

Table 9
Distribution of Humanitarian Aid Between Four Areas of Operation (per cent)

Area	*ICRC*		*UNICEF*		*WFP*		*Total*	
	1979-80	*1981*	*1979-80*	*1981*	*1979-80*	*1981*	*1979-81*	
Kampuchea	34	44	82	83	65	63	54	
Border	46	55	16	12	27	24		20
Thai camps	19				0		46	22
Affected Thais	1	1	1	5	8	12		4

There are several factors which affect these distributions in various agencies. In Kampuchea, there were other large aid donors, notably the socialist countries and the Western voluntary organizations. In Thailand

and at the border there was plenty of aid available from the voluntary organizations as well. In the Thai camps the role of the UNHCR was so prominent that there was no need for any direct involvement by UNICEF and the WFP.

The main criterion in deciding whether or not aid is to be given was information concerning the real needs for emergency aid. A common feature of all disasters is that, to begin with, little detailed information is available, but action is started urgently because it is more important to try to save lives than to write and read reports. An aid official in Kampuchea has described the situation as follows: 'Initially, we found the whole place in a hopeless situation, so it made sense to pour the aid in.'[20] If judged on the basis of the first holding centre, Sa Kaeo, the situation was chaotic in Thailand as well: 75% were malnourished, 20% severely malnourished, 26% suffered from cerebral malaria, 5% from TB, and dysentry and ulcerated sores were rife.[21] As a massive influx of refugees were expected – probably in a similar condition – it was only natural that the whole programme was started in an atmosphere of extreme urgency.

In the course of time, the problems became more clearly delineated and the whole operation took shape. As this programme developed into its tripartite structure, the aid agencies had to evaluate – after the initial phase – the aid needs of each three parts. Ideal, of course, would have been that the aid agencies would have had one single fund, which they could have distributed according to their own humanitarian and neutral criteria. Ideal management of a large operation would also require plenty of flexibility in the allocation of funds, as well as the possibility to transfer funds from one area or from one sector to another according to the development of the emergency. But these ideals are rarely possible – and certainly they were not possible in the case of Kampuchea. Instead, the donors usually gave funds separately for each agency and for each area of operation.[22] Funds allocated for Thailand, for instance, had to be used in Thailand.

As noted earlier, the refugee influx into Thailand remained much smaller than had been expected. In addition – and partly as an alternative to the Thai camps – new encampments emerged at the border which more or less resembled the military bases of Kampuchean political movements. However, these camps did not become very popular either – they too were dangerous, and people feared that they would be recruited into the armed units.

No documentation is so far available on how the aid agencies perceived the structure of this aid operation. The aid agencies' internal evaluations are confidential; nonetheless, these may be expected to be reflected in their budgets. Thus, if the actual humanitarian aid needs in Thailand and at the border differed from expectations, this should be seen in the budgets for the period after the initial phase.

The budgets of the ICRC, the WFP and UNICEF are compared in Table 10. The first column for each organization shows the actual percentage distribution of funds between various parts of the programme as reported

Table 10

Actual and Proposed Percentage Distributions of Aid Programme 1979-80

Area	*ICRC Actual Oct. 79-31.3.80*	*6 March[a] Proposed 1.4.80-[b] 31.12.80*	*21 March Proposed April-June 80*	*1 May Proposed April-June 80*	*Actual Jan. 1981*	*UNICEF Actual Oct. 79-31.3.80*	*6 March Proposed 1 April-31.12.80*	*21 March Proposed April-June 80*	*1 May Proposed April-June 80*	*Actual Jan.-1981*	*WFP Actual Oct. 79-31.3.80*	*6 March Proposed 1.4.80-31.12.80*	*21 March Proposed April-June 80*	*1 May Proposed April-June 80*	*Actual Jan. 1981*
Kampuchea	36	49	69	72	34	60	77	77	62	82	59	54	63	73	65
Border	29	28	31	14	46	27	17	19	28	16	31	28	30	15	27
Thai camps	18	22		13	19	—	0		—	—	6	10		5	—
Affected Thais	3	1	0	1	1	2	6	4	5	2	4	8	7	4	8
Other	—	—	—	—	—	—	—	—	5	—	—	—	—	3	—
(Payments for WFP)	14	0	—	—	—	11	—	—	—	—	—	—	—	—	—
Total	*100*	*100*	*100*	*100*	*100*	*100*	*100*	*100*	*100*	*100*	*100*	*100*	*100*	*100*	*100*

Sources: Calculated from *Humanitarian Operations . . .*, report prepared by the Inter-Agency Working Group, 6 March 1980, Annex III; Ibid., 21 March 1980, Addendum I, Annex; Ibid., 1 May 1980, Addendum I, Table 2; *Kampuchea Back From the Brink*, published by the ICRC, Geneva, October 1981, p.37.

[a] The date the report was published.
[b] Periods for which the budgets are made.

by the agencies themselves afterwords in March 1980. The second, third and fourth columns are percentage distributions *proposed* on 6 March, 21 March and 1 May. The fifth column for each organization is the actual percentage distribution in January 1981.

Analysis of the budgets shows clearly that all three agencies wanted to increase the share of Kampuchean aid after March 1980 from what it had been in the initial phase. The ICRC and WFP proposed a very high share to be given to Kampuchea in May. UNICEF also proposed a notable increase in the Kampuchean share of the operation in March, but for some reason it returned to its initial 60% level in its budget in May.

Comparison of these proposals with the final shares shows that UNICEF and the WFP used their funds more or less in accordance with their proposals, whereas the final use of ICRC funds is contrary to the direction proposed in its budgets; this may indicate that there were divergent views within the ICRC on the allocation of funds in this programme.

While the agencies clearly wanted to increase the share of aid to be given to Kampuchea, they just as clearly wanted to decrease the share of aid going to Thailand and to the border. Official reports shed no light on why this was the case. This may have something to do with developments noted earlier, i.e. the small size of the Thai refugee camps – as compared to expectations – and the overtly political and military role of the border zone, which made the monitoring of aid very difficult. At the border there was a great risk of aid going to military, political and black market purposes. Despite the difficulties at the border, however, it was not possible simply to exclude the border from the programme, since the civilians in this area were in a very difficult situation.

The Kampuchean people were still in need of emergency assistance in 1981, although the most acute phase had passed. The Joint Mission had officially ended in December 1980, but the same organizations continued. The three agencies used a total of US $ 120.7 million in 1981, which were used as shown in Table 11. The reason why the three agencies played no direct role in the Thai holding centres was that they were run by the UNHCR. As the number of residents was also decreasing rapidly, the ICRC, UNICEF and the WFP could withdraw and concentrate on more urgent humanitarian tasks. The ICRC used a greater share of its funds at the border than UNICEF and the WFP. In its budget for 1981, the ICRC had planned to use 48% of its Kampuchean funds for relief at the border, but the final share was 55%.[23] The presence of the ICRC is, of course, explained by its obligation to protect the victims of a military conflict.

To understand the magnitude of the humanitarian programme for the Kampuchean people, one has to take a closer look at the role of the bilateral donors and voluntary organizations as well. As Vietnam had been responsible for the political change in Kampuchea in 1979, the first deliveries of emergency aid were expected to come from her and her political allies, notably the Soviet Union. Although Vietnam's economic resources were

Table 11
Use of Funds in the Kampuchean Operation in 1981
(millions of US $ and percentages)

	ICRC		*UNICEF*		*WFP*		*Total programme*	
Area	*Jan.-Dec. 1981 $*	*%*	*Jan.-Dec. 1981 $*	*%*	*Jan.-Dec. 1981 $*	*%*	*Millions of US $*	*%*
Kampuchea	11.0	44	22.7	83	43.2	63	110.0	58
Border	13.8	55	3.2	12	16.7	25	33.7	18
Thai camps	—	—	—	—	—	—	34.6	19
Affected Thais	0.4	1	1.3	5	8.4	12	10.1	5
Total	*25.2*	*100*	*27.2*	*100*	*68.3*	*100*	*188.4*	*100*

Source: *Humanitarian Operations*, World Food Programme, November 1981, Annex II, Table 3. Figures for January-September are actual, for October-December estimated.
* Total funds by ICRC, UNICEF, UNHCR, WFP and FAO.

limited, she provided various types of emergency aid: over the period 1979-80 her aid amounted to US $ 118 million.[24]

The largest single bilateral donor, however, was the Soviet Union, whose aid in 1979-80 was worth US $ 219 million and in 1981 US $ 95 million. The value of aid from other socialist countries was estimated at US $ 48.9 million.[25] This makes the total value of bilateral socialist aid US $ 385.9 million in the first two years after the takeover of Phnom Penh.

For Western voluntary organizations, too, Kampuchea was a huge challenge to which they responded on a massive scale. The total value of their aid in Kampuchea in 1979-80 was about US $ 75 million, of which 45% came from the NGO-Consortium, while the share of WCC-CCA, CIDSE, ARRK and World Vision were 10-15% each. Within the NGO-Consortium, over one third of the aid was given by the British OXFAM. The next largest donors were the Lutheran World Federation, Deutsche Caritas, CEC, OXFAM America and Deutsche Welthungershilfe.[26]

The combined value of humanitarian aid given within Kampuchea by the socialist countries, the large Western aid agencies and private voluntary organizations in 1979-80 reached a staggering total of US $ 717 million. The value of aid from the socialist countries was higher than the Western aid in this phase: in 1981 the international aid agencies gave US $ 110 million while the value of Soviet aid was US $ 95 million.

The official reports on this aid programme have not, unfortunately, given as accurate information as the above on the role of bilateral donors and voluntary organizations in Thailand and in the border region.

The Impact of Humanitarian Aid in Kampuchea

At the outset of the aid programme, the Kampuchean people were short of everything. The aid agencies naturally concentrated on the most urgent task: to save lives by providing food and drugs. About half of the aid provided by the Joint Mission in 1979-80 consisted of food (see Table 12).

Table 12
Composition of Kampuchean Emergency Aid Provided by Joint Mission 1979-80 (millions of US $ and per cent)

Aid category	*$ million*	*Per cent*
Food	125.2	49
Agriculture, fisheries	41.0	16
Logistics	62.7	24
Health	9.3	4
Education	4.7	2
Operating costs	11.0	4
Miscellaneous	2.8	1
Total	*256.1*	*100*

Source: calculated from *Kampuchea Back From the Brink.*

For reasons mentioned above the first food aid shipments in 1979 came from the socialist countries. Vietnam, herself a poor country, has announced that she provided 100,000 tonnes of rice. Vietnamese provinces with high agricultural productivity were taxed for aid to Kampuchea. The official figure for Soviet food aid in 1979 is 159,000 tonnes.[27]

After a slow start, the large Western aid agencies tried to rush the first aid shipments through. Their first food aid shipments, some of which came from Europe, came in by air; later, shipments came mainly by sea. By January 1980 the Joint Mission had provided 40,000 tonnes of food aid. The first aid flights chartered by the voluntary organizations also contained mainly food and drugs. By June 1980, the NGO-Consortium had sent 13,400 tonnes of food. The WCC-CCA programme sent 6,000 tonnes of food in during the first three months of the operation.[28]

The aid donors soon came to realize that there were some particularly undernourished groups in Kampuchea who needed supplementary nutrition: thus, specially designed food packages were provided for hospitals, orphanages and schools.

By December 1980 the Joint Mission food aid totalled 278,642 tonnes and that of the Soviet Union 323,000 tonnes, adding up to a total of 601,642 tonnes in 1979-80. At the same time the Joint Mission had provided supplementary feeding kits for 650,000 persons. A large amount of feeding kits were also provided by the Western voluntary organizations.

In 1981 the large aid agencies still had to send 70,000 tonnes of food aid, and the Soviet Union sent 80,000 tonnes. In spite of all efforts at self-sufficiency, Kampuchea was still in need of food aid in 1982 due to erratic weather and lack of agricultural resources. Originally the UN agencies had planned to stop Kampuchean emergency aid in 1981.

The distribution of food aid was taken care of by the Kampuchean authorities, and monitored by the aid personnel by tours, by interviews of officials and aid recipients, as well as by actual supervision of the distribution in the warehouses and in the villages. Distribution being in the hands of the officials, there was some doubt as to the end-use of the aid; nevertheless, the aid agencies repeatedly stressed that no misuse of aid was found and that all aid went to civilians.

The agencies were – in fact occasionally concerned about the efficiency of distribution – although they could not discuss this matter in public. The Phnom Penh government seems to have been of the opinion that the peasants should feed themselves as much as possible – the imported food aid was mostly needed in the cities for people not engaged in agriculture. It was estimated that about one third of the food aid went to Phnom Penh and large amounts were provided for provincial capitals, in particular those located along the railway, roads and rivers. A large share was given to civil servants and workers, especially during the first months when the government did not have money and paid people with food. In June 1980 it was estimated that 70% of the food aid went to the cities. In the countryside food was given to particularly vulnerable persons such as widows or farmers who were not self-sufficient in food. Part of the food was collected into emergency stocks. In general food distribution was timed so as not to disturb planting or harvesting.

Due to the almost non-existent transportation network in Kampuchea in 1979, all aid donors had to pay special attention to questions to do with transport. The Joint Mission used US $ 62.7 million for the purchase of trucks, barges, tugs and cranes; also, tankers for fuel transportation were bought. Cars, motorcycles and bicycles were brought in, too, as Kampuchea did not have any means of communication. The socialist countries and the voluntary organizations also devoted much attention to problems of transport and communication.

The Joint Mission supplied 1,041 trucks and 192 Land-Rovers; the socialist countries some 1,700 vehicles; and the voluntary organizations 210 trucks and 11 cars. The spare parts and fuel had to be supplied as well.

River transport proved practical in a country where the rainy season complicates road transport, and makes even many of the main roads impassable. Many parts of Kampuchea could be more easily reached by river – including Phnom Penh. All aid donors contributed to the repair of the ports, and supplied barges, tugs and boats for river transport.

The aid to Kampuchea was shipped by air, by sea and through the 'unofficial' land-bridge from Thailand. A daily flight operated between Bangkok and Phnom Penh; unfortunately, the planes had to fly via Vietnam, increasing the time and cost of this vital service. The bulk of the aid was shipped by sea, however. Problems were here originally caused by the insufficient capacity of the key ports of Kampuchea, Kompong Som and Phnom Penh, but once new cranes, forklifts and competent staff had been moved in, things improved. Transportation from these ports onward by rail, trucks or barges was problematic too, and at times the aid piled up in the warehouses.

The railway transported 21% of the aid in Kampuchea: the aid agencies would have wanted to give more assistance here, but the aid donors did not consider repairing of railways as 'emergency aid'.

A further problem in transport was that relief goods had to be transported from Kompong Som to other provinces via Phnom Penh.[29] The aid agencies suggested that aid supplies to Western Kampuchea be arranged with truck convoys from Thailand. Referring to political and military problems the authorities in Phnom Penh never permitted this. The aid agencies therefore started the distribution of relief goods at the border for Kampucheans from the nearby provinces. At times this created a flood of traffic to the border and probably contributed to the strengthening of the border zone, thus probably causing much more destabilization in Kampuchea than truck convoys would have done.[30]

Agricultural production was naturally considered crucial for the survival of the Kampuchean people: the sooner productivity could be raised, the less the need for food aid. Estimates of cultivated area in 1979 differ broadly: while US satellite reports estimated that only 10% had been planted, another estimate was that 700,000 hectares had been planted. In normal years, the cultivated area had been 2.4 million hectares. In 1980 the government decided to double the cultivated area. All foreign aid donors regarded rapid and efficient agricultural rehabilitation as the only means to avoid widespread hunger in 1980. The international aid donors provided altogether 73,000 tonnes of seeds as follows: FAO 29,000; UNICEF 2,000; Vietnam 10,000; voluntary organizations 10,000; in addition, some 22,000 tonnes of seeds were imported via the land-bridge. If one calculates that 70 kg of seed are on average needed to plant one hectare, the aid was enough for slightly more than one million hectares.

The conditions for agricultural development were extremely poor: thus, fertilizers, irrigation equipment, tools and various chemicals had to be provided by the aid programmes. Because of the severe shortage of draught animals, the agencies had to make efforts to supply them, too, although it was not easy. Finally, the revival of agriculture suffered from the lack of skilled personnel able to advise in cultivation programmes and maintenance of machinery.

The Joint Mission's agricultural development programme was run by the FAO, which used US $ 36 million for the purpose, as well as assisted in fishing. Assistance from the voluntary organizations totalled US $ 30 million – this part of aid was their first priority (40% of their total programme). In spite of all efforts and a good harvest from over one million planted hectares, the FAO estimated the deficit after the 1980/81 harvest at 220,800 tonnes. Of this, international food aid was to cover 102,500 tonnes, the rest was expected from bilateral donors. The planting target for 1981 was 1.7 million hectares, but erratic weather again led to a notable deficit at the beginning of 1982.

The FAO originally intended to close the agricultural programme in 1981; however, because of difficulties in achieving self-sufficiency in food production, it has remained in Kampuchea. Its activities include soil improvement, animal care, local seed cultivation, post-harvest programmes and fisheries development. Some voluntary organizations are participating in these programmes, too.

The health situation in Kampuchea was also alarming in 1979; malaria, TB and parasites were common, and the situation was complicated by malnutrition. The voluntary organizations and the Joint Mission provided several hundred tonnes of drugs and medical equipment, and supplied hospitals, dispensaries and health posts. The ICRC provided five medical teams, and training programmes were initiated for local staff. Vaccination campaigns and other preventive care measures were taken, particularly to get malaria and TB under control. Projects were undertaken for the development of sanitation and hygiene. A new faculty was founded for medicine and pharmacy, and drug production – although on a modest scale – was started. In spite of the closing down of the Joint Mission in December 1980, both the ICRC and UNICEF stayed on in Phnom Penh in 1981. Their programmes included water projects, drug supply, medical equipment, blood services and expertise. Some voluntary organizations also continued health programmes, and socialist countries provided large amounts of aid for health care. Their aid included material aid, equipment, and experienced staff. The Soviet Union presented a new hospital to the country in Phnom Penh.

The system of education in Kampuchea had to be completely rebuilt. To reach as many children as possible, aid agencies financed by Western governmental sources focused all their efforts on primary education. UNICEF, in consultation with UNESCO, provided material for teacher training, textbook printing, as well as for reconstruction of schools. In addition, some voluntary organizations, such as the Catholic Consortium and the ARRK, participated in the attempts to restore education in the country. School children also received food and health services.

Due to their mandate for emergency aid only, the large Western humanitarian agencies could not include industrial development in their programmes, even though all manufacture was at a complete standstill. The socialist countries, as well as the voluntary organizations, tried to help some key industries back onto their feet. The voluntary organizations gave aid for a bicycle factory, for production of cotton goods for medical use, for production of medicines, textiles, fishing nets, shoes, soap and plastic utensils (such as plates, bowls and dishes); i.e. for the production of goods by which the basic needs of ordinary people could be satisfied. The socialist countries gave assistance for vocational education, construction, fertilizer production and rubber and cotton production.[31]

The huge humanitarian programme in Kampuchea required a large staff, but Kampuchean officials were originally opposed to the idea of having a big international staff in the country. This neverthless changed as time passed: in October 1979 the Joint Mission had only 11 representatives in Phnom Penh, increasing to 17 in December, 42 in February 1980 (as medical teams arrived), 56 in June, 69 in September and 71 in December 1980. The voluntary organizations' staff also grew from a handful at the outset to 15 in June 1980 and to over 20 at the end of 1980. The aid agencies, in turn, worked in close co-operation, and their activities were well co-ordinated all the time: field tours, for instance, were so arranged that more or less the entire country was covered.[32] At the beginning of 1982 there were still some 60 aid staff in Kampuchea, but the number has constantly decreased since.[33]

In 1981 UNICEF took part in the health care for mothers and children, as well as in the development of road and river transport. The ICRC remained to supervise the medical teams, but was willing to withdraw in 1982. The WFP stayed on because of the estimated food aid needs of 75,000-100,000 tonnes both in 1981 and 1982. The only international humanitarian agency to increase its involvement was the UNHCR, which started financing the programmes for returnees in Kampuchea. At the end of 1980 it planned to finance the return of 300,000 Kampucheans from abroad; at the end of 1981 it gave support for 370,000 returnees, 56,000 of whom had come back since January 1981.[34]

In the final judgement, the Kampuchean humanitarian programme has succeeded in its main task: to get the nation back onto its feet and save its people from death and starvation. Nonetheless, Kampuchea is still an extremely weak nation, and the need for long-term development programmes is vast. Ideally, development co-operation should be started immediately after the crisis is over. The Soviet Union has signed an agreement on long-term development co-operation with Kampuchea. On the other hand, Western development agencies, not wanting to recognize the present government which took power by force and maintains its power with foreign forces, have not been able to start development programmes.

The Impact of Aid along the Border and in Thailand

According to a recent comparative study of 33 refugee crises, a crisis can be considered large when the number of refugees exceeds 500,000, middle-sized if they number 100,000 - 500,000, and small if they number less than 100,000.[35] The conflict over Kampuchea caused, in this light, a *pressure* towards a large refugee problem, but most of this pressure was blocked along the Thai–Kampuchean border and only about a quarter were allowed to cross the border. If judged on the basis of the total number of dislocated Kampucheans in the border camps and in Thailand, the crisis was middle-sized.

But the sheer number of dislocated people is of course not the only criterion in determining how serious a crisis is – even a small crisis can turn serious if the influx of refugees is sudden and if they are in a poor way. When the Kampucheans started coming to the border and to Thailand, the relief agencies had every reason to believe that a massive influx of refugees was to be expected, all of them in a very bad way.

The border zone was about 10 km wide and controlled by the armed Kampuchean groups. All traffic was controlled by the Royal Thai army. To some camps – particularly in the northern and southern sectors – there was no access at all. The residents of the border camps were never properly registered; however, the experienced aid agencies had their own methods of counting the civilians in those camps they were allowed to enter.[36] Most of the time the border camp population was by and large equal with the number of residents in the Thai camps – or somewhat bigger.

All aid was intended for civilians, yet in the northern and southern zones it was the Thai army that made monthly relief orders. The WFP delivered the supplies to the frontier warehouses from where they were picked up by the army and distributed to cross-border feeding points; from here, teams of porters often carried the relief to the villages.[37] Many journalists and other observers have noted that aid distribution was clandestine – access to distribution stations was often denied for 'security reasons'. In the central zone, where the ICRC/UNICEF team was in charge of distribution, supplies were initially left to the camp authorities for distribution. Preliminary surveys were used to estimate the need, while the camp leaders gave the numbers of residents. However, the agencies soon learnt that these figures were deliberately inflated: part of the relief went to soldiers and the flourishing black market. In June 1980 the agencies started to deliver food rations for women only: on the basis of the demographic surveys each woman received 2.5 - 3.0 rations.

After occasional food and drug deliveries had been provided by UNICEF and the WFP in summer 1979, the ICRC and UNICEF assumed overall responsibility for the regular aid programme which began in October; the WFP was their important partner. Knowing the situation in the border zone, the aid agencies had to participate in all forms of activities in trying to ensure that aid went to civilians (see Table 13).

The Joint Mission used a total of US $ 102 million in 1979-80 for the border operation. The ICRC and WFP bore the main economic burden of this relief: they used US $ 45.5 and 44.0 million respectively in 1979-80, while UNICEF used US $ 13.7 million. Notable funds were also allocated by the voluntary organizations, whose aid was subordinated to ICRC/UNICEF co-ordination – which was not always an easy task. Most voluntary organizations interested in border relief were US based; some were qualified and experienced, but others were too eager in trying to promote their anti-communist and religious goals.[38]

Most of the food aid was provided by the WFP, but the ICRC and UNICEF also purchased large amounts. Distribution was in the hands of

Table 13
Breakdown of ICRC/UNICEF Aid Components at the Thai–Kampuchean Border (millions of US $ and per cent)

	ICRC				*UNICEF*			
Aid	*1979-80*		*1981*		*1979-80*		*1981*	
category	*$*	%	*$*	%	*$*	%	*$*	%
Rice seed					0.9	6		
Food, water	11.9	26	0.3	2	4.9	36	0.3	9
Logistics	5.2	11	0.5	4	3.3	24	0.5	16
Health	13.6	30	2.9	21	1.2	9	0.4	13
Education	—	—	—	—	—	—	0.2	6
Operating costs	9.6	21	6.0	43	2.4	18	1.0	31
Miscellaneous	5.2	11	4.1	30	1.0	7	0.8	25
Total	*45.5*	*99*	*13.8*	*100*	*13.7*	*100*	*3.2*	*100*

Sources: *Kampuchea Back from the Brink*, and *Humanitarian Operations*, World Food Programme, November 1981, Annex II, Table 3. Figures for January-September 1981 are as actually used, but for October-December 1981 estimated.

UNICEF and the Thai army, initially also the ICRC. Although the poor nutritional status of the population improved during the first months of relief, pockets of hunger and malnutrition remained. Supplementary feeding was provided for pregnant and lactating women, children, hospital patients and old people. As late as May 1980 nutrition surveys still showed that malnutrition among children had increased – it was precisely after these surveys that the agencies began stricter control of aid recipients. Demographic surveys, head-counts of women and nutrition surveys were carried out to ensure the impact of food aid. At times, the distribution was interrupted to improve the practices and attitudes of the camps leaders.[39] Some voluntary organizations participated in the feeding programmes, too.

Food and water transportation was an immense task. During the most intensive phase of the programme, an average 80-100 trucks left daily from the warehouses in Aranyaprathet to the border; an average 2,000 tonnes of relief supplies were transported every week. Also, water had to be brought in from Thailand almost every day. In May 1980 the Joint Mission hired 60 trucks and 36 water tankers for border relief.

Medical care was co-ordinated by the ICRC, which also supplied medical teams, drugs and other medical equipment. Mobile medical teams set out for the camps in the morning, returning to Thailand in the evening. Health posts were built in the main camps. Critical cases were transported to the surgical units in the Thai holding centres. Because of the fighting, many wounded patients had to be treated, too, and at times the health personnel could not reach the camps because of military activities. The ICRC also co-ordinated the health aid given by the voluntary organizations.

Medical supplies and drugs for border relief as well as for operations in the holding centres were provided from the ICRC pharmacies in Bangkok, Aranyaprathet and Sa Kaeo. The ICRC also started tracing missing family members, giving special attention to children. Unfortunately, the authorities in Phnom Penh did not co-operate in this service.

The border operation included social services and assistance for education. Orphans, abandoned babies and handicapped persons were taken care of. Educational material was provided for children between five and 16 years, and Khmer teachers were trained.

At the end of 1981 UNICEF was replaced as the leading agency at the border by the United Nations Border Relief Operation (UNBRO) which took charge of more or less the same activities (food, water, shelter, sanitation, health, social services and education). The WFP was still UNBRO's most essential agency; UNBRO also co-ordinated relief provided by the voluntary organizations.[40]

The voluntary organizations had important activities at the border: supplementary feeding, clinics for mothers and children, sanitation, vaccinations, education. As the large agencies gradually withdrew from the border, they handed their relief tasks over to the voluntary organizations.[41]

The ICRC, too, decreased its border activities in 1981, but continued to give medical help for the land-bridge people, and maintained a surgical unit in the Kao-I Dang holding centre plus two medical teams for the border camps. It co-ordinated preventive health care programmes and assisted in medical training programmes. In addition, it continued tracing and mailing services. It participated in the work of Border Medical Co-ordination Groups together with the American Refugee Committee, Concern, an Italian team and UNICEF, which co-ordinated the health work.

As far as the border camps are concerned, one may conclude that, despite the difficult conditions, the main task, to save the civilians trapped in a most dangerous area, succeeded. The creation of the border zone had been part of local power politics. Military activities in the area continue, as do black market activities. Access to some camps is still forbidden. As late as 1981, the agencies still had to repeat their demands for better monitoring of the relief, for better security of their personnel, and for a clear separation of civilian and military persons in the area.

There was evidently some manipulation of the camp populations as well, but detailed information as to how this was arranged is not available. Although information on the camp populations was never easily come by, the number of people in the camps controlled by the KPNLF (and to a lesser degree by the Moulinaka) seems to have increased between January 1981 and February 1982 by 37,800, whereas the populations controlled by the Khmer Rouge have changed little in size. This development coincides with the political goal of the leading Western powers to strengthen the political status of the KPNLF within the coalition of Kampuchean political groups.

Table 14
Changes in Border Camp Populations January 1981 – February 1982

Sector and camp	*Population January 1981*	*Population February 1982*	*Difference*
Northern Zone			
N1 Nam Yun (KPLNF)	1,000	2,500	1,500
N2 Chong Chom (Moulinaka)	2,000	2,000	—
N3 Khum Han (Khmer Rouge)	1,000	1,000	
N4 O'Bok (KPNLF)	6,800	1,500	5,300
N5 Ban Bara Nae (Moulinaka)	2,000	6,000	4,000
N6 Paet Um (Khmer Rouge)	15,000	14,000	1,000
N7 Naeng Mut (Khmer Rouge)	300	300	—
Central Zone			
NWla Nong Pru (Khmer Rouge)	8,000	8,000	—
NWlb Tap Prik (Khmer Rouge)	8,000	8,000	—
NW2 Ban Sangae (KPNLF)	6,618	11,000	4,382
NW3 Ban Samet (KPNLF)	35,724	44,500	8,776
NW7 Nong Chan (KPNLF & Moulinaka)	15,000	36,500	21,500
Southern Zone			
S2 Sok Sann/Kraduk Chan (KPNLF)	6,000	9,000	3,000
S3 Borari (Khmer Rouge)	19,000	19,000	—
S4 Nam Ta Luan (Khmer Rouge)	17,000	17,000	—

Sources: *Humanitarian Operations*, report prepared by the Inter-Agency Working Group, New York, 23 February 1981, Annex V and Table 6 p.50.

Because the civilians at the border needed relief, but at the same time the conditions for giving relief were so difficult, the UNHCR drew up a plan for assisting those Kampucheans who wanted to return to Kampuchea from Thailand, and particularly from the border. From the point of view of the civilians at the border – and considering the frustration of the relief agencies – this was the only sensible thing to do.

The land-bridge was an essential part of the border relief. It could be motivated by three humanitarian reasons: 1) the humanitarian agencies thought that the border provinces were not receiving sufficient relief from Phnom Penh; 2) by supplying aid at the border they supported normal life in the nearby provinces and thus reduced the flow of people moving permanently to the border; and 3) road transportation from Thailand was fast and cheap; border distribution was the best alternative after the Phnom Penh authorities had forbidden truck convoys from Thailand. Politically, then, this form of aid was favoured by Thailand and the United States.[42]

However, the land-bridge also had negative consequences: it drew people to the border, and strengthened the human 'security zone' between Thailand and Kampuchea. Also, some of the people who came to collect relief at the border did not return, but moved on to the camps. As it again became obvious that the monitoring of this aid was difficult and part of it was going to soldiers and the black market, the agencies tried to improve monitoring by registering the people and with surveys of their backgrounds and aid needs.

It was estimated that at least one third of the relief delivered through the land-bridge was lost.[43] What got through evidently relieved the food situation and hastened agricultural revival in the nearby Kampuchean provinces: in June 1980 the aid agencies estimated that 85% of the people came from Battambang, 4% from Siem Riep, 6% from Pursat and the rest from further away. Besides food aid and agricultural packages, much of the rice seed for planting in 1980 was delivered through the land-bridge. The ICRC and UNICEF stopped the land-bridge deliveries in January 1981, the main humanitarian argument being that the situation in the nearest Kampuchean provinces had improved so much that this form of aid was no longer needed. Nevertheless, as people had become used to the availability of relief at the border, they simply kept coming in.

After Thailand had opened her borders for Kampuchean refugees, many relief workers feared that a massive influx of more Kampuchean refugees would mean more chaos.[44] The UNHCR assumed overall responsibility for the holding centres, and quickly mobilized funds for the construction and operation of six centres for the Kampucheans. In 1979-80 it used US $ 85.8 million for the holding centres. About one fifth of this sum was transferred to the WFP for the purchase of food, the rest was used for shelters, water, sanitation, and other services. The ICRC took care of the medical work, for which it allocated US $ 18.7 million in 1979-80.

The people waiting at the border were transported to the holding centres by the Thai army. After Sa Kaeo, new centres were opened at Kamput and Khao I Dang, which became one of the largest with a population of 130,000 in May 1980. The first influx of arrivals – sick, dying and wounded – were remnants of the Khmer Rouge army and their supporters. Nevertheless, there were also educated people among the refugees, seeking a better life abroad after many years of suffering. It was quite commonly believed that it would be fairly easy to resettle in third countries from Thailand: in Western Europe, or in the United States. Thailand, too, expected the Western powers to take a large share of these refugees. But there was disappointment in store for most of the refugees and the Thai government: implementing increasingly strict immigration policies, Western countries did not accept a large-scale resettlement of the Kampucheans.

The refugee influx to Thailand caused widespread international concern. While the international mass media were making the problem known throughout the world, the appeals by the humanitarian organizations were well responded to by the public, and record funds were raised within a short time. Nearly all voluntary organizations wanted to make their contribution for the benefit of the suffering Kampuchean people. In December 1979, the peak of the programme, the number of Joint Mission staff in Thailand was 342, and the number of Thai Red Cross personnel 88; in addition some 400

people worked for the voluntary organizations. Thus, the operation had to co-ordinate the work of almost 1,000 people during the most intensive phase.

The impact of the aid programme soon became evident: mortality decreased, diseases were got under control, and the nutritional status of the refugees improved rapidly, thanks to regular food aid as well as supplementary feeding of the most vulnerable groups. Life in the holding camps soon settled down, and schools were opened for children. Special attention was paid to orphans and unaccompanied children. Missing parents and relatives were searched for – at the end of 1980, 1,413 children had been reunited with their families living in the holding centres (1,162), in the border camps (130), or overseas (121).[45] All necessary social services were arranged, and basic education was arranged in the Khmer language.

Due to the unexpected developments in the crisis (the border zone growing continuously while the Thai camps remained small), the agencies started reconsidering their role as early as March 1980. In May-June 1980, the first changes were made: the UNHCR started to co-ordinate health care with the assistance of voluntary organizations. The ICRC left most of the medical work to the voluntary organisations – the major exception being its surgical unit in Khao I Dang – but continued tracing and mailing services for the refugees. In 1981, tracing was also transferred to the UNHCR. At the end of 1981, the UNHCR also tried to get rid of its operative task, while keeping its role as a supervisor and co-ordinator. The number of Kampucheans in the holding centres in October 1981 was 90,000.

With the approaching rainy season and the diminishing refugee influx in 1980, the centres were rearranged to get through the rainy season. This led to the construction of more durable shelters and facilities for six centres.

Voluntary organizations had a notable role in the holding centres, participating in medical care, feeding programmes, education, water supply, sanitation and resettlement assistance. Accurate figures for their share of the assistance programme are not available; however, as an example we may mention that of the 100 tonnes of food provided for the centres every day in August 1980, 85 tonnes were given by the WFP and 15 tonnes by the voluntary organizations.[46] As a great number of aid agencies were involved in the aid programme, all operations had to be co-ordinated. They held their meetings in Bangkok every week, and European and US voluntary organizations also held regular meetings in Geneva and New York.

It is useful to point out that not all staff in Thailand worked in the Thai holding centres: the staff based in Thailand also took care of the border relief, as well as of the relief to Kampuchea – for example, half of the ICRC staff in Bangkok in 1980 was engaged in the delivery of relief to Kampuchea.

The humanitarian programme in the Thai holding centres succeeded well. In contrast with the typical refugee crisis, funds were sufficiently available, as the agencies had been prepared for a much more extensive programme. The appeals for assistance had raised plenty of funds, and governmental funds were also allocated in abundance.

It has been estimated that the conditions in the Thai holding centres were far better than in any other Asian refugee camps. In any case the holding centres were so well organized that the standard of living was in some cases better than in Thai neighbourhood – for instance the mortality rate in the holding centres was in 1981 lower than in the neighbouring areas. Thus, a programme for helping the local population was started – that is quite exceptional in international humanitarian aid operations. UNICEF, the WFP, the Thai Red Cross and the voluntary organizations still assisted the 80,000 affected Thais in 1981: assistance was given for health services, education, vocational training and feeding.

Conclusions

In 1979, the very existence of Kampuchea was at stake: society was destroyed, and its people faced the risk of premature death as a result of starvation, diseases, violence and sheer exhaustion.

The refugee problem came to be an essential part of the question in Kampuchea. Had this part of the crisis developed spontaneously, it would have caused a large refugee population in Thailand. But due to the strict Thai policy, the flow of refugees was to a great extent blocked at the Thai–Kampuchean border. The number of people pushing their way to the border increased rapidly since summer 1979 and they were in an extremely poor way, which of course caused added pressure on the humanitarian agencies. The most intensive emergency aid lasted for 15 months.

We started our analysis by asking *whether* the Kampuchean people were saved by the humanitarian programme. Without any doubt, this vast task was fulfilled: people survived in Kampuchea, at the border and in Thailand. However, the nation is still very weak, and as long as no permanent political solution is found to the problems, the risk for new emergencies is always present.

The question of *how* the people were saved is of secondary importance. However, the Kampuchean humanitarian programme was undertaken under so complex political conditions that it makes sense to ask this question, too. This operation being one of the most difficult ones ever undertaken, it could be used as a lesson for future humanitarian work in open political conflicts.

The assistance programme for the Kampuchean people started perhaps six to eight months too late. But once it finally did get under way, it definitely brought considerable relief. Good emergency programmes should often be followed by development programmes, however. In Kampuchea, only the socialist countries have been able to do this while the Western development agencies stay out because of political obstacles.

The border area was evidently the most problematic element in the aid

programme. The very creation of this human buffer-zone is most questionable, particularly because civilians were here used for military purposes. If they had to be stopped there, then why were not efforts made to separate civilian areas clearly from the military quarters and deliver aid only to them? The way the border area was arranged made the monitoring of aid impossible, and this benefited both soldiers and the black market.

The land-bridge part of the border relief was also contradictory. Although understandable as the most efficient and cheapest route to the western parts of Kampuchea – particularly if the Phnom Penh authorities neglected the needs of the border provinces – the land-bridge also had negative effects. It pulled people to the border like a magnet and strengthened the border zone – also questionable from the humanitarian point of view. A considerable share, perhaps one third or even more of the border aid went to waste or was misused, again because monitoring was impossible. Could this waste really be afforded? Was, in fact, the whole land-bridge operation a result of a too large relief programme?

The Thai part of the humanitarian programme was much smaller than had been expected. Why did the Thai government declare an open door policy and then eat its words? And why, promoting the border zone and having military control over the area, did Thailand not complete its role by separating the civilians from the military? This would have been in accordance with its other policies, as it expected the aid agencies to assist at the border if they gave assistance to Kampuchea.

From the point of view of the humanitarian organizations, the main problem is perhaps their insufficient independence. The very launching of the programme was delayed because of political pressures, and the agencies could not always allocate their funds according to their own, humanitarian criteria. The monitoring of aid delivery was difficult, sometimes impossible, because of political pressures. The agencies did not have access to all pertinent information in Kampuchea and in the border area – again because of political difficulties – and indeed they were not always able to make independent decisions as to the distribution of aid between various areas and functions according to their humanitarian grounds.

The Kampuchean programme raises serious questions: are international rules concerning humanitarian operations in open conflicts sufficient? Is the obligation to receive humanitarian aid in an emergency clear enough? Why are agencies not allowed to have all the information they need? How could they rid themselves of the political pressures of the parties to the conflict and their donors, so that they could follow their humanitarian criteria only? How could the position of the civilians be made more secure in modern conflicts?

Finally, the Kampuchean emergency as well as the humanitarian operation shows the power of the mass media both in its positive and in its negative forms. The positive impact was that international solidarity was raised so effectively that plenty of funds were available, and the emergency in 1979 and the even worse one that was threatening in 1980 were prevented.

The negative aspect, then, was that part of the information was pure propaganda, and humanitarian work also suffered from the propaganda in the press. The experienced humanitarian agencies operate in a neutral and discreet manner. Even if they are attacked in public, they do not make any public statements about the parties to the conflict, about the victims, about the donors, or about themselves.

Notes

1. *International Review of the Red Cross*, Vol.15, nos.167-71, 1975, information sections on external activities in each issue.
2. Statement by Gareth Porter, Institute for Policy Studies, in *Hearing before the Subcommittee on International Relations of the Committee on International Relations, House of Representatives, Ninety-Fifth Congress, First Session*, 3 May 1977. US GPO, Washington DC, 1977.
3. It is worth noting that the international aid agencies, notably the Red Cross and some UN organizations, co-operated with Thailand, Laos and Vietnam after 1975. Thus the rules and practices of these agencies were presumably very familiar to the Vietnamese authorities when the aid programme for Kampuchea was negotiated in 1979. Vietnam itself received humanitarian aid in 1978 because of the fighting at the Kampuchean border. Cf. the reports on external activities of the ICRC in Indo-China in *International Review of the Red Cross*, Vols.16, 17 and 18, 1976-8. The claim that the authorities in Phnom Penh did not know the rules of the ICRC and UNICEF in 1979 is therefore questionable.
4. Murray Hiebert and Linda Gibson Hiebert, 'Famine in Kampuchea: Politics of Tragedy', *Indochina Issues* 4, December 1979.
5. Ibid.
6. 'Background on UNICEF Participation in the North-West Border Operation', UNICEF, 15 July 1980 (unpublished mimeo).
7. Hiebert and Gibson Hiebert, op.cit., 1979.
8. 'Background on UNICEF', op.cit.
9. Cf. *Kampuchea Back from the Brink*, ICRC, Geneva, October 1981, pp.5-14.
10. The members of the Consortium were: AFSC, Community Aid Abroad, Brot für die Welt, Caritas International, Caritas Netherlands, CEBEMO, CNCD & Belgian FFH, Frere des Hommes, CRS, Deutsche Caritas, DWHH, CEC, Dutch Medical Committee, Frere de Nos Freres, Lutheran World Federation, Manitese, Methodist Relief Fund, Mennonites, Miserior, Novib, OXFAM America and Belgique, Help the Aged, OXFAM/UK and Quebec, Red Barna, Sol. Soc. de Belgique, Trocaire, World Relief, Australian Council for Overseas Aid, Euro Action Accord.
11. For more information on these aid programmes, see *IDOC Bulletin*, No.11-12, November-December 1980.
12. Hiebert and Gibson Hiebert, op.cit., 1979.
13. 'Background on UNICEF', op.cit.
14. Ibid.
15. *UNHCR* 5/6, December 1979-January 1980.

16. Interview of General Soonsiri, Secretary General of the Thai National Security Council, for the representatives of the Finnish Inquiry Commission, Bangkok, 11 March 1982.
17. Ho Kwon Ping, 'The Frustrations of Mercy'. *Far Eastern Economic Review*, 14 December 1979, pp.13-14.
18. Ibid.
19. External Activities, Asia. *International Review of the Red Cross*, Vol.19, No.213, November-December 1979, pp.321-4.
20. *International Herald Tribune*, 4 January 1982.
21. *UNHCR*, op.cit., p.17.
22. *Kampuchea Back from the Brink*, op.cit.
23. *Humanitarian Operations Arising Out of Developments in Kampuchea*, 23 February 1981, Annex VI, Table II.
24. *Humanitarian Operations*, op. cit., 10 November 1980; data provided for the Finnish Inquiry Commission by the Soviet Embassy, Phnom Penh, 1 March 1982.
25. *Humanitarian Operations*, op. cit., 10 November 1980.
26. Ibid., and NGO-Consortium–Kampuchean Members Contribution Summary, 31 December 1980 (mimeo).
27. Figures on Vietnamese aid by Britain–Vietnam Association, published in IDOC, op.cit., 1980, p.11. For Soviet aid, information provided by the Soviet Embassy in Phnom Penh.
28. Cambodia/Kampuchea, NGO-Consortium for Kampuchea, Bulletin No.12, 27 June 1980 and IDOC Bulletin, op. cit., 1980. At the outset of the programme, the NGOs sent plenty of food aid, but after the formation of the ICRC/UNICEF joint mission – and their commitment to send large quantities of food – the NGOs decided to concentrate on other needs, in particular agricultural development, transportation, supplementary feeding, reconstruction of small industry and fishing. See also *OXFAM: A Review of the Year 1979-1980*.
29. *Kampuchea Back from the Brink*, op. cit., 1981, p.20.
30. Cf. Special UNICEF/ICRC Mission to Kampuchea. Summary Cable Report, 7 May 1980.
31. *OXFAM: A Review of the Year 1979-1980* and IDOC Bulletin, op.cit., 1980.
32. *Kampuchea Back from the Brink*, op.cit., 1981; *Humanitarian Operations*, op. cit., 10 November 1980.
33. 'Personnel des Organizations Internationales En Poste Fixe', mimeo by the international aid agencies, Phnom Penh, February 1982.
34. *Humanitarian Operations*, op.cit., November 1981.
35. Cf. 'Harto Hakovirta, Valtioiden konfliktit, pakolaisvirrat ja pakolaisongelmat' (Conflicts, refugee flows and refugee problems), University of Tampere, Department of Political Science, Research Reports 67/1981, p.53.
36. See for example, *Demographic Survey*, UNICEF, Bangkok, 29 October 1981.
37. John McBeth, 'A Quiet Security Role', *Far Eastern Economic Review*, 23 January 1981, p.36.
38. Cf. John Pilger, 'The 'Filthy Affair' of Denying Relief', *New Statesman*, 12 October 1979, pp.46-7.

39. *Kampuchea Back from the Brink*, op. cit., 1981; UNICEF's Programme Responsibilities for the North-Western Sector of the Thai/Kampuchean Border from September 1979 to 31 December 1981', World Food Programme, Office of the Representative, Bangkok 1982 (mimeo).
40. 'Activities of the Border Relief Operation', WFP, Office of the Representative, Bangkok, 19 January 1982.
41. 'Activity of Border Voluntary Agencies', WFP, Office of the Representative, 16 February 1982.
42. Thailand wanted to see a strong buffer zone between herself and Vietnamese-backed Kampuchea. She promoted the land-bridge by, for instance, requiring no licences for seeds distributed at the border in 1980, whereas the FAO needed such export licences when it shipped seeds by air and sea to Kampuchea. See John McBeth, 'The Seeds of Survival', *Far Eastern Economic Review*, 2 May 1980, pp.22-4. The US Ambassador in Thailand, Morton Abramowitz, used his influence to increase land-bridge routes. In his letter to the Thai Prime Minister on 5 February 1980, he wrote: 'For some time I have been persuaded that the points now open for the delivery of food for transport into Kampuchea are insufficient in relation to the needs of the population inside that country. I believe it is in our common interest to create additional locations along the border.' He recommended a couple of new feeding points and suggested that the Thai Prime Minister use his influence on the ICRC/UNICEF on this matter. He also considered feeding of non-residents in Nong Chan and Nong Samet useful – both camps are controlled by the KPNLF.
43. Richard Nations, 'Salvation in the Black Market', *Far Eastern Economic Review*', 18 January 1980, pp.21-2.
44. *UNHCR*, op. cit., 1980.
45. *Kampuchea Back from the Brink*, op. cit., 1981.
46. *Cambodia Action Update*, Vol.1, No.15, 4 August 1980, p.9.

7. International Law and the Kampuchea Question

by study group led by Allan Rosas

Human Rights

The UN Charter creates the basis for agreements on human rights maintaining the principle of the advancement of respect for the human rights and basic freedoms of all people regardless of race, sex, language or religion. Based on this, the UN General Assembly has approved a total of 37 agreements and declarations on human rights. In addition the UN's special agencies, such as the ILO and UNESCO, have concluded numerous agreements concerning human rights.

The Universal Declaration of Human Rights can be considered one of the most important human rights norms which, in spite of its form as a declaration, has gained broad significance in terms of international law. The declaration was approved in 1948 without any opposing votes; and the basic rights and freedoms it grants have not been forbidden later in any international document.

The core of the system of human rights can be said to consist of an entity formed by the Universal Declaration of Human Rights and the human rights documents of 1966. These documents are the International Covenant on Economic, Social and Cultural Rights and the International Covenant on Civil and Political Rights as well as an associated Optional Protocol.

On the basis of this Protocol the Human Rights Committee may receive individual complaints directed against states that have adhered to the Protocol.

In the case of Kampuchea, however, the Human Rights Committee has not been competent to make an examination as Kampuchea has not adhered to the Covenant on Civil and Political Rights let alone to its Optional Protocol. Instead, the question of Kampuchea has been discussed in the UN Commission on Human Rights. Though being a political body, the Commission has through the years become involved in examining particular situations as well, notably those involving a consistent pattern of gross violations of human rights.

The UN Commission on Human Rights first took up the Kampuchean situation only in 1978. At that time it was decided to transmit to the Kampuchean government the Commission's documents which concerned the human rights situation in the country and the government was asked for its comments and observations on the matter.[1] The international system of human rights agreements thus reacted to the obvious violations of human rights by the Khmer Rouge regime in making them a subject of multilateral international discussion and in this way producing a condemnation of at least some degree. In 1978 the governments of Canada, Norway, Great Britain, the United States and Australia as well as Amnesty International and the International Commission of Jurists provided the Commission on Human Rights with weighty material on the human rights situation in Kampuchea.[2] The information had been gathered mainly from interviews with refugees and from Phnom Penh radio broadcasts. However, no broad investigation by a neutral international body had been carried out. Interviews with refugees are generally not very reliable and extreme descriptions may easily be considered as representative.[3] In the case of Kampuchea, however, the experiences of people from different parts of the country were in such conformity that they seemed credible and indicated that there had been gross violations of the international norms of human rights.

Kampuchea, just as all other states in the UN, is bound by the principles contained in the UN Charter and the Universal Declaration of Human Rights because these are considered generally accepted international norms of behaviour. In 1950 Kampuchea announced that it was becoming a party to the International Convention on the Prevention and Punishment of the Crime of Genocide. Similarly in 1957 it joined in the Convention on the Abolition of Slavery, the Slave Trade, and Institutions and Practices Similar to Slavery. The third agreement it is party to is the International Convention on the Elimination of All Forms of Racial Discrimination which it signed in 1966. Kampuchea is thus bound by some of the most central principles of human rights.

It can be said that the Pol Pot regime violated some of the most basic principles of the Universal Declaration of Human Rights. The basic right of people to life was violated on a wide scale and the individual was denied the basic security provided by the state. Torture was widespread especially in the prisons. Executions were cruel; arrests were arbitrary; there were no courts or process of law, and punishment was often carried out on the spur of the moment. Personal property was forbidden and there was no right to a private life. Marriage rights were restricted and the family did not receive sufficient social protection. The freedoms of religion and conscience were limited as were the freedom of opinion and the freedom of speech, and the exchange of information was made impossible. The Khmer Rouge did not permit the freedom of assembly or the freedom of association, and citizens were not able to move freely within the country. Citizens also were denied the right to choose their own place of employment, they were not paid wages, working days were extended and there was insufficient rest, food and medicine. In practice there were no schools and participation in the cultural life of society was impossible because it simply did not exist.[4]

In its reply to the charges presented within the UN Commission on

Human Rights the government of Democratic Kampuchea ignored the issue itself.[5] The answer, delivered in a note, sharply condemned the colonialists and imperialists, the worst of whom were considered to be the British. The government of Democratic Kampuchea claimed that the 'British-imperialists' are still extremely barbaric and cruel and in fact they themselves have no right to speak of human rights. The UN furthermore should consider whether to permit imperialists and those practising expansionist policies to continue to interfere in the internal affairs of other countries and to use the UN as a forum to disseminate the logic of exploiters.

It was also stated in the reply that the intention of the imperialists was to encourage rebellion in the country, that they were leading a campaign of slander against Kampuchea with the aim of isolating the country, and that they wanted to prevent Kampuchea from solving its difficult problems including the acquisition of food for the population. Concerning the claims of murders, the government of Democratic Kampuchea said that this was slander by the imperialists and annexationists.

Thus the official statements by Democratic Kampuchea contained neither a real denial nor an admission that there had been widespread violations of human rights, but rather they were a polemical counterattack intended to call into question the motives for the accusations. The government of Democratic Kampuchea considered the creation of a new society as quickly as possible more important than human rights.

After the overthrow of the government of Democratic Kampuchea, its Foreign Minister, Ieng Sary, admitted that the official policy of the Khmer Rouge had been to liquidate opponents of the government, but he said that he himself was innocent and ignorant of the murders. He also noted that at the same time as people were undernourished Kampuchea exported rice in order to demonstrate its self-sufficiency. Sary estimated that 30,000 Kampucheans died from want or by execution. But he blamed the provincial leaders, claiming that they were agents of the Vietnamese whose purpose was to sabotage the government.[6]

Since 1979 the dominant theme in the handling of Kampuchea by the Commission on Human Rights has been the demand for the withdrawal of foreign forces from the country rather than violations of human rights. Various governments, most importantly the parties to the conflict, Democratic Kampuchea, Vietnam and China, presented the Commission with plentiful material accusing one another of mass executions, starvation, the destruction of the production mechanism, misuse of humanitarian aid and so forth. Confrontations in power politics are directly reflected in the work of the Commission on Human Rights. In 1980 and 1981, formally balanced resolutions were approved which stressed the principle of Kampuchea's right to self-determination and condemned human rights violations which had occurred while, however, emphasizing that the maintenance of human rights cannot be an excuse for violations of other people's human rights. These resolutions were not approved unanimously for the specific reason that the political barb was aimed at a condemnation of Vietnam for its actions in Kampuchea.[7]

It can be said that the international implementation of the human rights system was relatively ineffective in easing the Kampuchean situation. As often before in similar situations the machinery of human rights was slow moving and it was frequently bothered by a selectivity determined by political purpose. The most gross violations began to be over by the time the matter was brought to the Commission on Human Rights for consideration. The UN General Assembly did not handle the Kampuchean question before 1979, or at that time as a question of human rights, but rather as a violation of the sovereignty of a member state.

The international system of human rights does not necessarily function very logically; the same matters and the same principles appear in many agreements, but it easily becomes a problem as to what agreement should be the most important and what should be applied in which case. Likewise there is no clear formula as to what section of the agreements should be applied in any given situation. Is the most important position held by the UN General Assembly, the Security Council, the Economic and Social Council or the Commission on Human Rights? The organs of the UN are open to one another in their relations in settling human rights questions; they do not hold very strictly to their own sphere of activities, so there is substantial interaction. On the other hand a slowness caused by continuity can be discerned. The same questions are placed on the agenda time and time again.

The agreement-bound system of human rights thus functions in such a manner that on the one hand there is a certain minimum level, and on the other hand a certain consensus, on the breadth of violations that leads the system to react. The system of human rights should, however, react more readily and more individually than at present, so that even less wide-scale violation would be given attention. In the case of Kampuchea it was not until the substantiation of genocide that the human rights system was moved to action. In addition to everything else, because of the delay, consideration of the matter took place at a time when troops of a foreign country had already entered Kampuchea and the entire handling of the human rights situation was coloured by this fact. Furthermore, the character of the human rights situation in Kampuchea had changed: it was necessary to consider the consequences, a solution to the refugee problem, and the reconstruction of the country.

Despite a certain redundancy and ineffectiveness, the UN's system of human rights does have an important significance: it can reveal the various dimensions of complicated issues; it can also search for alternative solutions on the level of principles even if they do not lead to solutions in practice. In the main, the UN system gives only recommendations: perhaps the greatest significance of the UN has been that it has forced the international community as a whole to take a stand on issues.

Intervention

The military actions directed towards Kampuchea during the 1970s give cause for a consideration of the events in terms of international law. The concept of intervention and the question of the legality of interventions form a central real and judicial problem in efforts to prevent wars and strengthen the state of peace. Legally, the problem is worsened by the fact that interventions and other similar military interference lie somewhere in the grey area between international (between states) and internal conflicts. Under prevailing international law the use of force in relations between states is forbidden. On the other hand, international law does not directly outlaw civil wars (but it does contain some regulations for reducing the human suffering caused by them).

The concept of intervention has not received a completely unambiguous content of meaning in either international law or politics. In the following it is limited to concerning military interference in the internal affairs of another state. It can be considered typical of interventions that they are of short duration and that they are not so much aimed against another state, but rather against some power grouping. Especially in UN practice, the concept of intervention is regularly linked to situations in violation of international law.

The following three levels can be distinguished in military actions between states: 1) attack/occupation; 2) intervention; 3) military assistance.

The first level is emphatically connected with wars between states. The third level is connected to situations in which one state militarily aids the government of another state without breaking the norms of international law. Separating interventions from these two levels is often problematic. Hereafter the concept of military action is used to describe situations which are difficult to place in the three part division noted above.

According to Article 2 point 4 of the UN Charter: 'All members shall refrain in their international relations from the threat or use of force against the territorial integrity or political independence of any state, or in any other manner inconsistent with the Purposes of the United Nations.'

This rule is generally viewed as forbidding all use of aggressive force. On the other hand the following are permitted: 1) military sanctions decided by the UN Security Council in accordance with Chapter VII of the Charter; 2) self-defence alone or in concert with another state in the event of an armed attack.

According to Article 2 point 7 of the Charter: 'Nothing contained in the present Charter shall authorize the United Nations to interfere in matters which are essentially within the domestic jurisdiction of any state or shall require the Members to submit such matters to settlement under the present Charter, but this principle shall not prejudice the application of enforcement measures under Chapter VII.'

This rule forbids primarily the UN to 'interfere' in the internal affairs of its member states. The area of internal affairs has shrunk somewhat along with the expansion of the field of international law. For example, respect for human rights is no longer solely the concern of the authorities of the state in question.

Although according to its wording Article 2 point 7 of the Charter is aimed at the UN itself, it can be considered as an expression of a more general principle of non-interference.[8] The reference at the end of this regulation to Chapter VII of the Charter gives reason to assume that it also means military interference. The regulation, however, also bans other kinds of interference than military (e.g. various blockades).

Since the Charter came into force the UN General Assembly has approved a significant number of resolutions intended to reinforce and to adjust the precision of the ban on the use of force contained in the Charter. In this connection reference can be made to the resolution concerning interventions of 1965, the Declaration on Friendly Relations of 1970 and the definition of the concept of aggression of 1974.[9] The ban on the use of force also has a central position in e.g. the Final Document of the CSCE (Helsinki Agreement 1975).

With the exception of the UN Charter, the aforementioned documents are not state treaties. However, they do express to a large extent prevailing international law and its authoritative interpretation. At the same time they demonstrate the central importance which the UN and the international community places on the ban on the use of force. Even if those sections of the declarations which concern armed interference in a civil war by outside states are open to interpretation, they can lead to a very limiting attitude toward the legality of such operations. In terminology the declarations take the approach that situations which are defined as 'intervention' are against international law.

According to the traditional view, military assistance to a 'legal government' is permitted, but similar aid to 'rebels' is forbidden. The basis for this view is that aid to a legal government with its own permission does not mean the use of armed force against the state which that government represents. Conversely, sending troops to help rebels fight against the legal government means at the same time the use of force against the state in question. This latter situation is avoided, however, if the outside power recognizes the rebels as belligerents; in this case it is bound to maintain its neutrality in relations with both belligerents.[10]

The difficulties of objectively defining a 'legal government' and 'rebels' as well as the attempt to limit the use of armed interference have led to a view according to which at least wide scale military interference in a civil war on behalf of either side should be forbidden.[11] The other extreme is the view put forth according to which assistance to either side should be allowed.[12] Thus, roughly the following three choices of interpretation have been obtained:

1) military action on behalf of either side in a civil war is with at least certain conditions permitted;

2) such action is permitted only if it is carried out on behalf of the legal

government;
3) at least wide scale military action on behalf of either side is forbidden regardless of which party is considered the legal government.

The first of these is intended to coincide 'realistically' with the prevailing facts. It is not, however, in line with the norms of judical policy maintained by the international community. The aforementioned documents (including the UN Charter) are clearly based on the principle that military interference is forbidden if it can be viewed as being directed against a state proper. Nor in state practice have even the great powers in situations of intervention brought forth the view that intervention should be permitted regardless of which side it benefits. On the contrary, the government or grouping receiving the assistance has regularly been proclaimed the legal government or otherwise legitimate authority and consequently its opponents have been proclaimed rebels or representatives of a foreign power. The debate has centred more on which party is to be considered the legal government.

As one reservation to the above, mention must be made of the doctrine concerning wars of national liberation. Since the 1960s numerous resolutions have been approved, mainly through the action of the UN General Assembly, according to which wars of liberation are justifiable wars and even military assistance to liberation movements is permitted. The doctrine is mainly limited, however, to obviously colonial wars (Angola, Guinea-Bissau, Mozambique) or comparable situations (South Africa).[13] Indications or efforts to expand this to cover situations of civil war are apparent in, for example, the current US administration's designation of rebels in Afghanistan as 'freedom fighters' (thus making it possible to explain military assistance in line with the aforementioned UN doctrine).

In this connection, reference must also be made to the concept of humanitarian intervention. It has long been viewed that a state can carry out a limited intervention mainly to rescue its own citizens even if this does not happen at the request of the legal government An extremely cautious approach to this doctrine has been taken, especially in light of the UN Charter.[14] Recent state practice gives reason to ask whether an intervention which is unlawful according to its premise becomes lawful in exceptional cases in which it is used to end gross violations of human rights.

The third choice noted above (at least a wide-scale intervention can be unlawful regardless of on behalf of which side it occurs) can be regarded as desirable in terms of peace policy. This stand has been represented by, for example, the Institute of International Law (Institut de Droit International) and also similar positions have been taken in the literature of international law. Still, it can hardly be considered as an expression of valid legal-political norms. During the 1970s and 1980s outside powers sent armed forces or military experts to take part in civil wars or other similar situations in, among others, the following cases: Vietnam, Laos and Kampuchea (United States and Vietnam), Bangladesh (India), Angola (South Africa, Cuba), Uganda (Tanzania), Central African Republic (France), Chad (France and Libya), Afghanistan (Soviet Union) and El Salvador (United

States). In these situations neither the political opposition of the states involved in the operations nor other states have categorically suggested that the operations would be ipso facto unlawful completely regardless of the status of the power grouping receiving the military assistance. Even so, there can be seen in the reactions of the international community a growing tendency to dispute the legality of wide scale military action even if it can be described as taking place with the consent of the legal government.

The conclusion seems to remain, however, that the above mentioned second choice of interpretation (military action is permitted only if it occurs on behalf of the legal government), in spite of its deficiencies, still offers a judicial point of departure for an appraisal of military intervention. This model for interpretation is in best accordance with the official arguments of the states.

Thus it seems that what is meant by 'legal government' is basically to be understood as the regime in power. The more the position in power of the government is dependent on external (the support of a foreign state) rather than internal factors, the closer is the idea that military incursion invited by a puppet government is aimed against the state in question which that 'government' or something similar may not effectively represent. If, on the other hand, the grouping in power commits on its territory the kind of mass destruction that can be characterized as genocide and so violates those obligations it undertook by joining in the international human rights agreements, thus forfeiting its representative status, then the possibility cannot be entirely excluded that the threshold for legal interference would lower. These dimensions are fundamental in an examination of the Kampuchean question.

On 18 March 1970 the military government of Lon Nol came to power in Kampuchea. On 30 April the Americans and troops of the Saigon government entered the eastern parts of Kampuchea with the official goal of destroying the bases and logistics routes of the North Vietnamese. Following the two-month operation, participation in the events in Kampuchea continued in the form of wide scale aerial bombings. Aerial bombings had also taken place before the events of 1970. The entry of ground forces into Kampuchea did not occur at the invitation of the Lon Nol government. On the other hand this government did not present a protest over the operation, but rather seemed to have approved it to a quite great extent afterwards.

The arguments presented by the United States on behalf of the legality of the operation concentrated on two main questions:[15] firstly, reference was made to the traditional right of neutrality (neutrality in time of war) according to which a neutral state (Kampuchea) is obliged in line with its possibilities to prevent the use of its territory for military operations or bases; in the US view, the inability of the state of Kampuchea to prevent the presence of North Vietnamese troops and bases in the eastern parts of the country gave the other belligerents the right to limited interference.

Secondly, the United States admitted that the UN Charter partially places the traditional right of neutrality in a new light. However, it took the view that the operation fulfilled the demands of Article 51 of the Charter on the use of collective self-defence. The US presence in South Vietnam was based on the principle of collective self-defence (the defence of South Vietnam from an attack by North Vietnam); the wide scale presence of North Vietnamese troops in Kampuchea thus gave the United States and South Vietnam the right to direct military actions against the territory of Kampuchea as the latter was unable to prevent them. Reference was also made in the arguments of the United States to the fact that, at least afterwards, the Lon Nol government approved of the operation by ground forces.

An evaluation of the military action mentioned is, in legal respects, closely tied to the judicial nature of the entire Indo-China war and the behaviour of the United States in the overthrow of Sihanouk. The event cannot thus be evaluated solely in terms of the traditional right of neutrality. The status of this principle has become rather unclear in view of the UN Charter and state practice. Additionally it must be noted that the old principle has been viewed as requiring the existence of a 'war'; the conflict in Indo-China did not necessarily constitute a 'war' in the formal sense. It is obvious that in such armed conflicts as the one in Indo-China, those states remaining outside the war do not have an absolute obligation to observe traditional neutrality in all its parts. The assistance they supply to states which have come under attack is at least to a limited degree lawful.

If the military presence of the United States in Indo-China (particularly in South Vietnam) is viewed as unlawful, then it is clear that the operation of 30 April 1970 in Kampuchea was also unlawful. If the US presence in South Vietnam is viewed as lawful, it is still possible to consider as unlawful, for example, the operations aimed against North Vietnam and Kampuchea. In the case of Kampuchea this would be because the operation exceeded the legal limits of self-defence as it meant the use of armed force against a foreign state which had not been guilty of carrying out an armed attack in the sense of that noted in Article 51 of the Charter. The situation is complicated by the claimed consent of the Lon Nol government for the operation. The apparent participation of the United States in the overthrow of the Sihanouk government makes the relevance of this consent at least questionable.

The intention in this connection is not to take a stand on which of the above choices or formulas is best in harmony with 'prevailing law'. However, the example does illuminate those difficulties that a legal analysis, just as much as a political or moral evaluation, unavoidably runs up against in this kind of situation – in which the international and internal aspects of a conflict are intertwined in such a complicated manner. Similar points of view also fit the wide scale bombings carried out by the United States in Kampuchea. In their case, the question also arises of an evaluation of the bombings and the application of human rights in armed conflicts. In that they hit the civilian population they are basically in violation of the rules of war concerning the protection of the civilian population. These rules were codified in 1977 in a protocol to the 1949 Geneva Conventions on the protection of the victims of war.[16]

In December 1978 Vietnamese troops and some troops of Kampucheans opposed to the Pol Pot regime crossed the border to begin a wide scale operation to overthrow the administration of Pol Pot. Phnom Penh fell on 7 January 1979: the next day the People's Revolutionary Council was formed under the leadership of Heng Samrin. The number of Vietnamese troops has been estimated at a minimum of 200,000. The size of the force of Kampucheans accompanying them seems to have been rather small, although the estimates are affected by the indistinct nature of the divisions between various national and ethnic groups in Indo-China. The entry of these forces had been preceded by an uprising in the eastern parts of the country, its suppression, and a border war between Kampuchea and Vietnam.

The armed arrival of Vietnam seems, on the basis of the UN Charter, an undeniable use of force. Even if Kampuchea can be considered as having been guilty of skirmishing on the border, it is clear that this did not justify the other party, under the principle of self-defence, to undertake as wide scale an offensive as that in question. Nor does Vietnam seem to base its argument solely on the principle of self-defence.

Another possibility would be to view the interference as lawful in that it occurred at the request of the 'legal government' (Heng Samrin). It is true that traditionally the 'legal government', as earlier noted, has been mainly understood to mean the government in power, regardless of the history of its origin or its policies. In this connection it can also be noted that the troops of Heng Samrin do not really seem to have established any actual administration on the territory of Kampuchea before the interference by Vietnam and that armed clashes between them and the troops of Pol Pot were few before the events mentioned.

The analysis can also, however, include the concept of humanitarian intervention. Traditionally it has been used to mean mainly a limited involvement by an outside state in a conflict for the rescue of its own citizens (an example of this type is the Entebbe operation). In light of the UN Charter, however, a very cautious attitude has been taken towards the concept of humanitarian intervention which arose during the age of imperialism. However, along with human rights regulations, the concepts of the universality and the general applicability of human rights have strengthened. On the matter of state practice, mention can be made of, for example, the occupation of Germany by the Allies in 1945 and from more recent happenings India's, Tanzania's and France's operations in East Pakistan (Bangladesh) and Uganda and the Central African Republic respectively. In the light of these and the situation in Kampuchea it can be asked if wide scale, gross and basic violations of human rights comparable to genocide justify, in some exceptional circumstances, a deviation from the ban on the use of force contained in Article 2 (4) of the Charter.

This conclusion can be reached by two routes: first it can be viewed that a Pol Pot type of repressive government is not in fact entitled to represent the state and people in question. Then, intervention to overthrow it is not aimed against the state which for a certain interval would have no legitimate government. This kind of formulation would require the principle of national self-determination to be adapted to demand of the country's élite a sense of responsibility and 'democratic' legitimacy exceeding a certain minimum level. Similarly the situation in South Africa is seen as being in conflict with the principles of human rights in that the majority of the people is even formally excluded from participation in the decision making process. It is clear that these types of formulations are not easy to adapt to the traditional state and power-centred international order. It can even be claimed that they only offer a formulation in international law for the defence of military interference. But still, the rise to the fore of human rights and basic freedoms as well as the right to national self-determination since the Second World War gives reason to seriously consider the relevance of these formulations to a judicial analysis of so-called humanitarian interventions.

A different formulation (which does not exclude the former) starts from the concept of a kind of international emergency. Then, it could be viewed that, for example, the entry of Vietnamese troops into Kampuchea was in violation of Article 2 (4) of the Charter, but that a pressing emergency (genocide) justified disregarding this norm on behalf of a greater good. At the same time, however, it must be stressed that the ban on the use of force is considered a very central and 'compelling' current norm of international law that cannot be disregarded on the basis of promoting other interests.

The actions by both the United States and Vietnam can be considered in terms of their justification as violating international law. They cannot, however, be criticized in the same manner. It can even be argued that at least the illegality of the interference by Vietnam cannot be considered completely undisputed. This is indeed weakened by the fact that the grounds of Vietnam's action were more political than humanitarian. If again the principles of human rights and self-determination are used as a basis for consideration, attention must be given to Vietnam's behaviour following its military action. The organization of Kampuchea's social conditions and administrative system is still, however, underway. The drawing of exact conclusions on the judicial aspects of the conflicts are thus not only difficult, but perhaps premature.

International reactions in this case have been rather forceful; the attitude of especially the non-aligned nations has been quite negative. The majority in the UN seems to consider that Vietnam's action was against international law. In the resolutions of the UN General Assembly the concept of intervention has been used and they have included condemnations of military interference in the internal affairs of Kampuchea and demands for the immediate withdrawal of foreign forces from the country.[17]

The resolutions of the General Assembly do not mention Vietnam or any other country by name – it is obvious, however, that the parts related to intervention are aimed specifically against Vietnam. A significant number of the non-aligned nations voted in favour of these resolutions, and this reflects their concern over the consequences for the international state system and governments in power of military interventions based on humanitarian purposes. On the other hand it is significant that reference is made in the resolutions to human rights and the rights of the Kampuchean people to 'democratically' choose their own government. These parts of the resolutions can be seen as a small step towards the legitimacy formulation sketched out above based on respect for human rights and the right of national self-determination.

The attitude of opposition to interventions especially among the non-aligned nations which has been expressed in the handling of the Kampuchean question has also been seen in their voting behaviour on representation at the UN. By supporting Democratic Kampuchea in questions of credentials they have at the same time taken a stand on intervention and against it. Also, discussions on the Kampuchean situation in the Commission on Human Rights have largely centred around the concept of intervention, while actual human rights aspects have, in recent years, remained in the background.

Representation in the UN

The representation of Kampuchea in the UN General Assembly is an issue which appeared during the years 1970-5 and again since 1979. During the first period, this was a question of the right of the Lon Nol government to represent the country in the UN despite the counter-claims of the deposed government of Prince Sihanouk. Since 1979 it has been a question of the validity of the credentials of the Pol Pot government which are challenged by the Vietnam-supported Heng Samrin government.

The characteristic marks of a government are usually noted as being effective control, independence and stability. Absolute demands for the express recognition of governments cannot be set. Many states (including Finland) have established the practice that the actual act of recognition concerns only states, not governments.[18] On the other hand, a state cannot completely avoid stands on the government issue in other states. The maintenance of relations by one state with the government of another can be viewed as an indirect 'recognition' of it as the legal government of that state.

This view gains increased weight in international organizations in which member states, by joining the organization, give approval to the membership rights of the other member states and thus also to their right to presentation in the work of the organization.[19] In UN practice it is stressed that the formal recognition of a government is not a requirement for its representation in the organization. On the other hand, this cannot be considered as a formal act of recognition.[20]

A distinction between a formal or actual act of recognition and an indirect cognition that the government (or state) exists as an objective fact, plays a part in clearing up the situation.[21] An example of 'cognition' is offered by the approval of the credentials of the governments of member states in international organizations.

The question of a member state's right to use its membership rights in the UN arose especially in connection with the issue of China (1949-71).[22] The right of the Peking government to represent China was rejected until 1971, starting in 1961 this being based on a principle formulated by the General Assembly according to which the question of changing China's representation was a so-called important question which required a two-thirds majority in the assembly. This stand has been criticized on the grounds that it gives too strong a position to the grouping whose credentials have been earlier approved.

Similarly the problem of two governments has appeared in the cases of the Congo (1960) and Yemen (1962). In the Security Council the question of the representation of the Congo was left open in September 1960 (Kasavubu vs. Lumumba) while in November the General Assembly approved in a vote the credentials presented by President Kasavubu. In the case of Yemen the representatives of the royalist government were permitted in the autumn of 1962 to temporarily participate in the work of the General Assembly which subsequently approved the credentials of the republican government.

While the cases noted above concerned rival governments, in 1956 the question arose of the right of Hungary's new government to represent the country in a situation in which there was no rival government to present its own credentials to the General Assembly. At the initiative of the United States the credentials committee and the General Asembly refused to take a position on the validity of the credentials of the Hungarian government from 1956 to 1962. Because its credentials had not been specifically rejected, Hungary was in practice able to take part in the work of the General Assembly. The situation was the same for South Africa from 1970-4. In the latter year, however, the General Assembly interpreted the situation in such a way that the delegation sent by South Africa's white minority government was not permitted to participate in the work of the General Assembly.

As for Kampuchea,[23] during the years 1970-4 the dispute concerned the representation of the Lon Nol government in the UN. In 1970-2 the credentials of the Lon Nol government were approved in the credentials committee and in the General Assembly after a debate. In 1973-4 proposals to return the rights of the 'Royal Cambodian Government of National Union' (GRUNK) in the UN were defeated in General Assembly votes. In 1975, with the fall of the Lon Nol regime, the right to representation automatically shifted to the new government.

A new phase in the representation of Kampuchea in international organizations began in 1979. For the years 1979-83 the credentials committee and the General Assembly continued to approve the credentials of Democratic Kampuchea. In 1979 and 1980 a proposal by India with reference to the country's unclear situation that Kampuchea's place be left temporarily empty was taken under consideration as a worthwhile alternative.

The dispute concerning Kampuchea's credentials in the UN General Assembly has shown that it is difficult to consider the question of credentials as merely a matter of procedure. In certain situations the question of credentials undeniably falls back on the question of the representation of a member state in the UN and the associated matter of the legal government of this state (in relations with the UN). In UN practice no clear difference has been made between the question of credentials and the question of representation.

UN practice strengthens as such the distinction which is made in the doctrine of international law between the question of representation and the actual recognition of a government. On the other hand, practice shows that these two questions affect each other in the determination of stands by other states. The attitudes of member states towards the representation of Kampuchea in the UN General Assembly have been clearly influenced by their general position regarding the various Kampuchean parties and their polities of recognition in this respect.

The bases which have been used in seeking a solution in the UN General Assembly during the years 1973-4 and 1979-83 can be divided roughly as follows: 1) effectiveness of control; 2) continuity; 3) territorial integrity; 4) human rights, democracy.

The first of these points means control of territory and administrative effectiveness. The second point refers to the preference which is given to the grouping which has earlier been in power. The third point is connected with the mood opposing intervention, and the fourth point concerns cases in which the democratic legitimacy of a certain grouping can be brought into question mainly because of violations of human rights.

The traditional view has been largely based on the demand for effectiveness. Already, earlier other, more 'subjective' criteria such as independence and democracy had been brought into the discussion. This feature seems to be gaining ground in UN practice. For example, in the case of Kampuchea the question of effective control has come up in General Assembly discussions, but at the same time attention has been emphatically placed on the question of intervention (point 3) and the question of mass destruction and the representation of the Pol Pot government (point 4). Thus, tensions are to be seen between the ban on force and intervention on the one hand, and the advancement of human rights and democracy on the other.

This feature was not yet very evident in the discussions on the status of the Lon Nol and Sihanouk governments in 1973-4, which in part can be explained by the fact that foreign interference (USA) was not then as massive in terms of ground forces as was the operation by Vietnam in 1978-9, and that the aspect of mass destruction was not given as much attention as during the Pol Pot period.

As for the debate carried out in 1979, it can be said that the intervention aspect gained a position of priority among the majority of UN member states. At the same time the continuity argument has played a certain part in the continuing approval of Pol Pot's credentials. This view also came forward in the approval of the credentials of the Lon Nol government during 1973-4.

The Kampuchean situation during the Pol Pot period, and the 1979 credentials debate, do not provide a basis for giving crucial weight to the view on continuity. A worthwhile alternative in this kind of situation may be to leave the state without representation in the UN for a temporary period. An example of this exists in the case of the representation of the Congo during the so-called Congo crisis. This alternative has been put forth also in Kampuchea questions during different phases in the UN, although it has not been approved by the majority of the General Assembly.

In principle the UN should allow its member states the right to representation. However, the organization can be seen as having the duty of making sure that there exists a power grouping which can be said to represent the state in question internationally at least to some reasonable degree. Considering a temporary period it is possible that the state entirely lacks this kind of government.[24] UN practice concerning the cases of Hungary and South Africa also speaks to some extent on behalf of this position. Even though there were no rival governments, doubts within the UN were directed towards the validity of the credentials signed by the governments in question (in the case of South Africa these credentials were even rejected).

Even if it is viewed that the right to representation can be withdrawn from a member state because of an unclear situation in the country, this manner of approach cannot last long. It can be asked if the principle of effectiveness combined with the principle of respect for human rights and democratic representation should not be given more weight today than the principle of continuity and the principle banning intervention.

Notes

1. Commission on Human Rights decision 9 (XXXIV), 8 March 1978. See also Note by the Secretary-General, E/CN. 4/1295, 6 June 1978 and Report of the Sub-Commission under the Commission on Human Rights, Note by the Secretary-General, E/CN. 4/Sub. 2/414, 14 August 1978.
2. Submission from the Government of Canada under the Commission on Human Rights decision 9 (XXXIV), E/CN. 4/Sub. 2/414/Add. 1, 14 August 1978; Submission from the Government of Norway under Commission on Human Rights decision 9 (XXXIV), E/CN. 4/Sub. 2/414/Add. 2, 18 August 1978; Submission from the Government of the United Kingdom of Great Britain and Northern Ireland under Commission on Human Rights decision 9 (XXXIV), E/CN. 4/Sub. 2/414/Add. 3, 17 August 1978; Submission from the Government of the United States of America under Commission on Human Rights decision 9 (XXXIV), E/CN. 4/Sub. 2/414/Add. 4, 14 August 1978; Statement submitted by Amnesty International, a nongovernmental organization in consultative status, E/CN. 4/Sub. 2/414/Add. 5,

15 August 1978 and Submission from the International Commission of Jurists under Commission on Human Rights decision 9 (XXXIV), E/CN. 4/Sub. 2/414/Add. 6, 16 August 1978. Further Submission from the Government of Canada under Commission on Human Rights decision 9 (XXXIV), 8 September 1978 and Submission from the Government of Australia under Commission on Human Rights decision 9 (XXXIV), 20 September 1978.

3. See *Amnesty International Report 1975-1976,* p.137; 'Prepared Statement of Gareth Porter', Hearing before the Subcommittee on International Organizations of the Committee on International Relations House of Representatives Ninety-fifth Congress, Washington, 3 May 1977 and David Boggett, *Economic and Political Weekly*, 5 May 1979, p.816.
4. Analysis prepared on behalf of the Sub-Commission by its Chairman of material submitted to it and the Commission on Human Rights under decision 9 (XXXIV) of the Commission of Human Rights, E/CN. 4/1335, 30 January 1979.
5. Note by the Minister for Foreign Affairs of Democratic Kampuchea, addressed to the Commission of Human Rights, E/CN. 4/1295, 13 June 1978 and telegram dated 16 September 1978 from Minister for Foreign Affairs of Democratic Kampuchea, addressed to Sub-Commission on Prevention of Discrimination and Protection of Minorities, E/CN. 4/Sub. 2/414/Add. 9, 20 September 1978.
6. Elizabeth Becker, 'Interview with Ieng Sary', *Far Eastern Economic Review*, 7 August 1981.
7. Resolution 29 (XXXIV), 1980, The Commission of Human Rights. See also Report of the Sub-Commission on Prevention of Discrimination and Protection of Minorities on its 32 session, E/CN. 4/1350, 3 October 1979; Draft Report of the Commission on Human Rights, E/CN. 4/L. 1501/Add. 7, 13 March 1980; The Situation of Human Rights in Kampuchea, Note by the Secretariat, E/CN. 4/1437, 19 January 1981.
8. Cf. Hans Kelsen, *The Law of the United Nations*, New York, 1951, pp.769-70; Leland M. Goodrich, Edvard Hambro and Anne Patricia Simons, *Charter of the United Nations, Commentary and Documents*, third and revised edition, New York, 1969, p.63.
9. Resolutions 2131 (XX) of 1965, 2625 (XXV) of 1970 and 3314 (XXIX) of 1974.
10. See Erik Castrén, *Civil War*, Helsinki, 1966, pp.117-19, 200-10.
11. See Resolution III/1975 adopted by the Institut de Droit International, *Annuaire*, Vol.56 (Session de Wiesbaden 1975), pp.544-9.
12. In this direction Tom J. Farer, 'Intervention in Civil Wars: a Modest Proposal', *Columbia Law Review 1967*, pp.266, 272; and 'Harnessing Rogue Elephants', in *The Vietnam War and International Law*, Vol.2, Princeton, 1969, p.1111, who, however, restricts his proposal for the legitimation of assistance to both incumbents and rebels to 'assistance short of tactical military support'.
13. On the concept of wars of national liberation see, e.g. Allan Rosas, *The Legal Status of Prisoners of War*, Helsinki, 1976, pp.262-6.
14. See Ian Browlie, 'Humanitarian Intervention', in *Law and Civil War in the Modern World*, ed. by John Norton Moore, Baltimore, 1974, pp.217-28. Cf. Richard B. Lillich, 'Humanitarian Intervention: A Reply to Ian Brownlie and

a Plea for Constructive Alternatives', in ibid., pp. 229-51.
15. John R. Stevenson, 'United Nations Military Action in Cambodia: Questions of International Law', *Depart of State Bulletin*, 62 (22 June 1970), pp. 765-70.
16. Dietrich Schindler and Jiri Toman, *The Laws of Armed Conflicts*, second revised and completed edition, Geneva, 1981, p.535.
17. Resolutions 34/22 of 1979 and 35/6 of 1980.
18. Hans Blix, 'Contemporary Aspects of Recognition', *Recueil des cours* (Académie de Droit International) 1970 II, p.647; Joe Verhoeven, *La reconnaissance internationale dans la pratique contemporaine*, Paris, 1975, pp.90-1.
19. See *United Nations Juridical Yearbook 1964*, pp.225-6, *1967*, p.320, *1970*, pp.170-1, *1977*, p.191; Henry G. Schermers, *International Institutional Law*, Alphen aan den Rijn, 1980, pp.126-8.
20. See a report by the UN Secretary-General concerning the representation of China in the UN, doc. S/1466; *United Nations Juridical Yearbook 1970*, p.170.
21. Blix, pp.609, 625-31, 689-95; D.P. O'Connel, *International Law*, second edition, London, 1970, Vol.1, p.128. See also Hans Kelsen, ed. by Robert W. Tucker, *Principles of International Law*, second edition, New York, 1966, pp.405-9.
22. See Schermers, pp.128-32.
23. UN General Assembly Official Records 1970-75 (25th-30th Sessions), 1979-82 (34th-37th Sessions). See also UN documents A/8142, A/8625, A/8921, A/9195, A/9230, A/9254, A/9779, A/9875, A/34/500, A/35/484, A/36/510.
24. Blix, pp.649-51, 690-1.

8. The Question of Kampuchea in the Mass Media

by study group led by Mikko Valtasaari

Kampuchea was dragged into the Indo-China war when the administration of Prince Sihanouk was overthrown in a coup by Lon Nol in 1970 and the United States extended expanded military operations into Kampuchea. The mass media as well had to take a stand on the turn the war had taken and to examine on the one hand the legality of the Lon Nol group and on the other that of the government-in-exile formed by Sihanouk.

The expansion of the war sharpened criticism by the major liberal press of the US against the policy of the President. For example, *International Herald Tribune* columnist Anthony Lewis stressed that the bombings in Kampuchea had no legal basis and he considered the operation as a corruption of the ideals of the US Constitition.[2]

Criticism of the bombings was based on various views. There were those who criticized them as militarily unfounded, those which saw no moral basis for the continuation of the war, and those who condemned them in the style of the Soviet press as 'the new aggression of imperialism'. If the attitude of the newspapers under study was overwhelmingly negative about the bombings, the question of the legality of the government sitting in Phnom Penh more clearly divided opinion.

The major liberal press of the United States, accompanied by international opinion, labelled the Lon Nol government as 'corrupt' and thus to some degree a questionable wielder of power. Even so, the *New York Times* supported the decision by the United Nations when it rejected China's proposal on naming the Sihanouk government as the representative of Kampuchea in the world organization. The *Times* wrote in December 1973 that the General Assembly had no reason to recognize a government-in-exile instead of a sitting government. [3]Later, the *Washington Post* defended deliveries of emergency aid to Lon Nol who was being rocked by pressure from the Khmer Rouge on the grounds that many Kampucheans still supported him.[4]

Immediately following the coup by Lon Nol, China became the patron of the Khmer Rouge: thus it promptly took a stand on behalf of the government-in-exile in the question of legality. In the public press Sihanouk received the attention accorded heads of state until 1973,[5] after which Khieu Samphan seemed to have that right. During those times Sihanouk had criticized the Khmer Rouge; the Chinese press was naturally quiet about this.

The Yugoslavs also at first gave their backing to the Sihanouk government-in-exile – it had, after all, followed a policy of non-alignment. The Belgrade weekly, *Politika*, even noted that Sihanouk had said that he would remain independent of both China and the Soviet Union.[6]

In 1973 a peace treaty concerning Vietnam was made and the guns were also silenced in Laos. The Kampuchean Khmer Rouge, however, refused to negotiate with Lon Nol. Prestigious observers such as Henry Kamm of the *New York Times*, Jack Anderson and the columnist pair of Evans and Novak incorrectly blamed Hanoi for the obstinacy of the Khmer Rouge.[7] It was only later during the same year that Kampuchean refugees told of battles between the Khmer Rouge and the North Vietnamese.

Commentary on the events of this period in Kampuchea was scarce in both the East and the West. When the Khmer Rouge were on the threshold of victory in the spring of 1975 deliberation on the coming direction Kampuchea was to take became current. The newspapers of China and the Soviet Union welcomed their victory as a 'liberation' and characterized them as patriots who reaped a well earned victory in a legitimate struggle for independence.[8] Belgrade's *Politika* celebrated Sihanouk, Khieu Samphan and the doctrine of non-alignment as the victors.[9]

Upon marching into the capital, Phnom Penh, the Khmer Rouge began immediately to empty it of inhabitants. Observations were received from eyewitnesses on the scene — information was limited only to this because a news blackout fell over Kampuchea affecting just as much the country's citizens as outsiders. The reasons and conditions for the evacuation of the cities remained for some time without explanation; in time it was discovered that a social system of a special nature had been created in the country. The mass media had to take a stand how to view the 'liberators' of Kampuchea.

Those who had best understood United States policy on Indo-China found it easy to digest this stunning information. Observers who had criticized US military policy also began to present pessimistic appraisals, but only a while later, a good half a year after the 'liberation'. In the Hong Kong *Far Eastern Economic Review,* William Shawcross stressed the responsibility of the United States for these events by saying that:

> U.S. Secretary of State Henry Kissinger has on several occasions since April lamented that an 'atrocity' is being perpetrated on the Cambodian people. Perhaps on this occasion he is not being deceptive; the life of ordinary people today really is appalling. He should however be reminded that the atrocity did not begin in April – it simply entered its sixth year. For five years the Cambodians had been abused by outsiders, principally the North Vietnamese and the Americans. By his obdurate personal refusal to encourage any sort of settlement (in the face of pleas from his own embassy in Phnom Penh), Kissinger must bear some measure of responsibility for the plight of the Khmer People today.[10]

In any case there was pressure for a re-evaluation of affairs: many observers who had formerly defended the justification of the revolutionary resistance in Indo-China reappraised their stand.[11] Both the conservative American columnist, William Buckley Jr. and liberal Democratic Senator George McGovern, recommended military intervention in Kampuchea for the return of human rights.[12]

Some critics of the Vietnam war such as Noam Chomsky and Edward Herman tried to defend the justification for their criticism with a kind of counterattack. In their work *The Political Economy of Human Rights* they attempted to bring into question the motives of the information media concerning the cruelties in Kampuchea.[13] Reports in the mass media and above all important statements about the 'red terror' were subjected to a critical review of sources. Furthermore, it was claimed that the gloomy reports on Kampuchea served the goals of the West's great power politics because similar violations of human rights by allies of Western countries (e.g. East Timor) did not get the same publicity.

This kind of self-examination is not practised in a more authoritarian environment. The closest ally of the Khmer Rouge, China, was allowed to send a delegation of journalists into Kampuchea immediately after 'liberation': no reports, however, appeared in the newspapers. Not until the second anniversary of 'liberation' were Chinese readers given an evaluation of the situation: the *People's Daily* wrote, *inter alia*.

> We were full of wonder at seeing their heroic deeds in defending and building the country. The cadres were closely in contact with the troops and refused sleep and food. The troops were changing nature night and day.[14]

An adoration of hard work and self-denial were a part of Chinese idealism especially during the time of the Cultural Revolution. The quote was thus written seriously.

In China, official policy directs reporting in the mass media in fine detail. China had indeed continuously supported the Khmer Rouge, but positive writings were delayed because of the internal power struggle within the Kampuchean leadership. When Pol Pot secured his position in 1977, news material in the Chinese press increased. In October 1977 Pol Pot made an official visit to China, declared himself the pupil of Mao Tse-tung and at the same time gained the unreserved support of China.

The Soviet *Novoje Vremja* took a stand on the 'red terror' for the first time in 1977. At that time the paper refuted reports in the Western media of genocide.[15] Writings about atrocities began to appear in the Soviet press as the confrontation between Kampuchea and Vietnam heated up.[16] And, in contrast, a few articles began to appear in the Western press which expressed an understanding of Kampuchea's agricultural reforms and its original, isolationist social policy. Questions of human rights were not then centrally in evidence. To what extent the increasingly strained relations between Vietnam and Kampuchea and their connection with great power politics could be seen in this kind of emphasis is still an open question.

The doctrine of non-alignment – which is a part of the nation's official foreign policy – obliged the Yugoslav mass media to handle Kampuchea carefully. At the same time they were able to benefit from the privileged relations granted by Democratic Kampuchea to Yugoslavia as an amiably disposed country. The first eyewitness descriptions of Pol Pot's Kampuchea were received specifically from the Yugoslav mass media.

A Belgrade television report presented in many countries was sufficient to register the peculiar scenes of Kampuchea without separate commentary. It showed a deserted capital in which money was blown by the wind down the streets, agricultural collectives in which there was no sign of family life, toil on the sites of dike construction which brought to mind the ages of the construction of ancient Angkor, and factories and production facilities in the hands of obviously untrained children. It put across a picture of an ideal turned into a nightmare, but nothing was told of the atrocities. The questions which the television report aroused were more clearly written in a five part series which appeared in *Politika*. In this series the writer appraised the cost paid for the revolution as too high even if the starting point were taken into account. He also doubted the ability of the system created in the country to carry through national construction, and he doubted in general the available official information.[17] The writer made these evaluations in his own name. Other news coverage of Kampuchea followed the official friendly line.

During that time the supply of information from Kampuchea was scarce and, for example, the Finnish media simply did not publish news or appraisals of the situation. The situation did change when Kampuchea became involved in a border conflict with Vietnam.

Hostilities between Kampuchea and Vietnam became public knowledge at the end of 1977. With the overthrow of the Pol Pot regime the information media began to consider whether Vietnam's action in Kampuchea was justified because of the violations of human rights which had occurred, or because Kampuchea had undertaken hostilities against Vietnam, or whether Vietnam was to be condemned as an aggressor which did not respect national borders. There was a conflict between human rights and the respect for sovereignty required under international law. Vietnam had made various co-operation agreements with the socialist camp and was therefore considered an ally of the Soviet Union: did this affect the appraisals?

Loyalty towards Vietnam in the conflict put an end to the restraint which had been evident concerning commentary on Kampuchea in the Soviet public media. It was explained that Pol Pot was acting on behalf of China and was responsible for the war. It was typical of Soviet commentary that the groupings to be opposed were seen as the extensions of either Chinese or US foreign policy, and so Pol Pot was viewed, just as Lon Nol had been previously, as carrying out specifically the policies of these hostile states. On the other hand, the Soviet mass media made no mention of the participation of Vietnamese troops in the overthrow of Pol Pot and characterized the event as a just uprising by the people against a tyrannical government.

Soon, note was taken of the cruelties which had been carried out in Kampuchea: in January 1979, *Pravda* estimated that three million Kampucheans met their deaths as the victims of the Khmer Rouge.[18] In reply to a reader who wondered why nothing had been told earlier about the affairs in Kampuchea, *Novoje Vremja* wrote that the Kampuchean government had been able to hide its deeds.[19]

The Yugoslav press staunchly supported official policy which is based on solidarity with non-aligned nations. When the situation in Indo-China was taken up at the non-aligned nations' summit in Havana in 1979, *Politika* did report the views of Cuba and Vietnam on the situation, but it removed the figure of Vietnamese Prime Minister Pham Van Dong from the photograph of participants in the meeting.[20] On the other hand, a Yugoslav commentator who did in fact condemn Pol Pot as a 'phenomenon of extremity' called for the joining together of all forces for a guerrilla struggle to drive the Vietnamese out of Kampuchea. According to him the problem was not local, but rather international.[21]

The leading Western information media generally condemned the incursion by Vietnamese troops, even though they also strongly disapproved of the atrocities instigated by Pol Pot. For example, the *International Herald Tribune* explained its stand on the issue by saying that just as the US action in Vietnam could not be justified by the nature of the competing governments, Vietnam's incursion could not be blessed by pointing to the nature of the Pol Pot dictatorship, and the paper wrote that the entire international community loses something when international borders are violated.[22]

William Buckley Jr, however, remained consistent: contrary to dominant opinion, he considered the arrival of Vietnamese troops justified for humanitarian reasons. In his view the condemnation of Vietnam's action expressed by President Jimmy Carter reflected a fawning approach towards China.[23]

Concern in the Western press caused by Vietnam's action was not always really based on solely moral viewpoints. The French *Le Monde* feared that the conflicts in Indo-China would spread to the rest of Southeast Asia.[24] The balance of power in the area had changed when Vietnam gained a foothold in Kampuchea; it was surmised that this is what Vietnam was primarily aiming at.

Most of the Western mass media did not consider the entry of Vietnamese troops into Kampuchea as justified: the return of human rights did not justify a disregard for national sovereignty. Hence the major part of public opinion shifted in a way behind Pol Pot. Mainly the Soviet media and media otherwise bound to Soviet views took a different stand on the matter, although at first these ignored the violations of human rights in Kampuchea.

In some other connections, for example Tanzania's action of sending troops into Uganda, the greatest part of public opinion seems to approve of this procedure. This case did not affect the balance of power in global politics.

When Kampuchea was dragged into the Vietnam war, US South-east Asia policy was already broadly a target of harsh criticism. The media of the socialist camp and the non-aligned nations which were bound to their countries' official views did not see anything acceptable in US actions. Also a large part of the Western media which otherwise had a positive attitude towards US policy condemned it on moral grounds. Of course there were those who understood the US government's line of action, but even their belief was gnawed by doubt. The Vietnam war had increased the prestige of the international system of morality and justice at the expense of the logic based on power politics.

With the final overthrow of the clients of the Unites States, it was gradually revealed that in 'liberated' Kampuchea human rights were not respected. Those who understood US military policy were the first to condemn them. The doubters were at first silent, but later had to express condemnation of the Khmer Rouge regime. The events were explained, however, as being partially a result of US policy and they warned against exaggerating the negative features in the new Kampuchean administration which at that point were poorly documented. The information media in the socialist countries, in non-aligned Yugoslavia and in China were silent about the atrocities, explaining them as slander.

When clashes began between Kampuchea and Vietnam, the Soviet information media and the media bound to its line revealed human rights violations and the tyrannical nature of the Pol Pot regime; apparently loyalty towards Vietnam removed the earlier barrier. In China and from the non-aligned countries, Pol Pot met with understanding.

The entry of Vietnamese troops into Kampuchea was interpreted in most of the Western press, as well as in the public media of China and Yugoslavia, as a violation of Kampuchea's sovereignty. On the other hand it can be viewed that it meant salvation for the human rights of the Kampucheans: two basic principles were in conflict.

Intervention on behalf of human rights received understanding only in the mass media of the socialist countries where the operation was not interpreted as an intervention, but rather as fraternal assistance; others condemned Vietnam's action. The stands of the media were largely divided according to whether or not the assessor felt solidarity with the Soviet Union and socialist camp.

Vietnam's incursion into Kampuchea finally split the broad understanding which concerned the morality of international politics and its adaptation in evaluating the events in South-east Asia. Appraisals again reflected the division in great power politics.

The attitudes of both power groupings towards the problems of Kampuchea thus went through numerous sharp changes during the 1970s, always according to how the entire situation in Indo-China and Kampuchea developed, and according to how they felt that these changes affected their interests. These interests affected the kind of picture that was given by the information media of each grouping even when it was a question of evaluations of the extent of, and reasons for, the human emergency which afflicted Kampuchea.

Notes

1. The subjects of examination have been some of the major Western newspapers (*New York Times, Washington Post, International Herald Tribune, Le Monde, The Times, Dagens Nyheter, Svenska Dagbladet*), the Soviet press (mainly *Novoje Vremja* and *Pravda*), the mass media of China, and as a representative of the non-aligned countries the mass media of Yugoslavia.
2. *International Herald Tribune*, 31 May 1973. The title of the article, 'Crimes of State', emphasizes the moralistic point of departure for Lewis' critique.
3. *New York Times*, 10 December 1973.
4. *Washington Post*, 6 February 1975.
5. E.g. in a report of 23 March 1970 by Xinhua on the programme declaration of Sihanouk's government-in-exile.
6. *Politika*, 15 October 1975.
7. *New York Times*, 10 March 1973; *New York Post*, 23 March and 5 May 1973.
8. *Pravda*, 23 April 1975.
9. *Politika*, 15 April 1975.
10. *Far Eastern Economic Review*, 2 January 1976. Later the writings of many other liberal observers including Anthony Lewis contained the same tone, *International Herald Tribune*, 28 December 1976.
11. See for example François Ponchaud, *Cambodge Année Zéro, Paris, 1977* and Jean Lacouture's article in *Le Nouvel Observateur*, 28 February 1977.
12. *International Herald Tribune*, 14 July 1977.
13. Noam Chomsky and Edward Herman, *After the Cataclysm: Postwar Indochina and the Reconstruction of Imperial Ideology*, South End Press, 1979, which is the second volume of a two part study entitled, *The Political Economy of Human Rights*. The same theses are presented by Denmark's Torben Retböll in his book *Kampuchea och den vestlige pressen 1975-78* (Kampuchea and the Western press), Copenhagen, 1979.
14. Xinhua, 17 April 1977.
15. Juri Antoshin in *Novoje Vremja*, No.44, 1977.
16. Valerian Skvortsov in *Pravda*, 14 January 1979.
17. *Politika*, Nos.19.3., 20.3., 25.3., 28.3. and 31.3., 1978. The Kampuchea series was written by Dragoslav Rancic.
18. *Pravda*, 14 January 1979.
19. Juri Tavrovski in *Novoje Vremja*, No.9, 1979.
20. *Politika*, 4 September 1979.
21. M. Mitrović in *Medjunarodna Politika*, 16 December 1980.
22. *International Herald Tribune*, 10 January 1979.
23. *International Herald Tribune*, 18 January 1979.
24. *Le Monde*, 10 January 1979.

RUTH AND VICTOR SIDEL
The Health of China:
Current Conflicts in Medical and Human Services for One Billion People
Hb and Pb

BETSY HARTMANN and JAMES K. BOYCE
A Quiet Violence:
View from a Bangladesh Village
Hb and Pb

REHMAN SOBHAN
The Crisis of External Dependence
Hb and Pb

ELISABETH CROLL
The Family Rice Bowl
Food and the Domestic Economy in China
Hb and Pb

W.F. WERTHEIM AND MATTHIAS STIEFEL
Production, Equality and Participation in Rural China
Pb

SRIKANT DUTT
India and the Third World:
Altruism or Hegemony
Hb and Pb

CONTEMPORARY HISTORY/REVOLUTIONARY STRUGGLES

SUMANTA BANERJEE
India's Simmering Revolution:
The Naxalite Uprising
Pb

WILFRED BURCHETT
The China, Cambodia, Vietnam Triangle
Pb

SELIG HARRISON
In Afghanistan's Shadow:
Baluch Nationalism and Soviet Temptation
Hb and Pb

MUSIMGRAFIK
Where Monsoons Meet:
History of Malaya
Pb

LAWRENCE LIFSCHULTZ
Bangladesh: The Unfinished Revolution
Pb

SATCHI PONNAMBALAM
The Tamil Question
Hb and Pb

HUMAN RIGHTS

PERMANENT PEOPLE'S TRIBUNAL
Philippines: Repression and Resistance
Pb

JULIE SOUTHWOOD AND PATRICK FLANAGAN
Indonesia: Law, Propaganda and Terror
Hb and Pb

RELIGION

KIM YONGBOCK
Minjung Theology:
People as the Subjects of History

WOMEN

BOBBY SIU
Women of China:
Imperialism and Women's Resistance, 1900–1949
Hb and Pb

ELSE SKJONSBERG
A Special Caste?
Tamil Women in Sri Lanka
Pb

GAIL OMVEDT
We Will Smash this Prison!
Indian Women in Struggle
Hb and Pb

AGNES SMEDLEY
Portraits of Chinese Women in Revolution
Pb

MARIA MIES
The Lacemakers of Narsapur:
Indian Housewives Produce for the World Market
Pb

ARLENE EISEN
Women in the New Vietnam
Hb and Pb

ELISABETH CROLL
Chinese Women
Hb and Pb

PATRICIA JEFFREY
Frogs in a Well:
Indian Women in Purdah
Hb and Pb

WOMEN IN THE THIRD WORLD: TITLES FROM ZED PRESS

BOBBY SIU
Women of China:
Imperialism and Women's Resistance, 1900–1949
Hb and Pb

INGELA BENDT AND JAMES DOWNING
We Shall Return:
Women of Palestine
Hb and Pb

MIRANDA DAVIES (EDITOR)
Third World – Second Sex:
Women's Struggles and National Liberation
Hb and Pb

JULIETTE MINCES
The House of Obedience:
Women in Arab Society
Hb and Pb

MARGARET RANDALL
Sandino's Daughters:
Testimonies of Nicaraguan Women in Struggle
Pb

MARIA MIES
The Lacemakers of Narsapur:
Indian Housewives Produce for the World Market
Pb

ASMA EL DAREER
Woman, Why do you Weep?
Circumcision and Its Consequences
Hb and Pb

RAQIYA HAJI DUALEH ABDALLA
Sisters in Affliction:
Circumcision and Infibulation of Women in Africa
Hb and Pb

MARIA ROSE CUTRUFELLI
Women of Africa:
Roots of Oppression
Hb and Pb

AZAR TABARI AND NAHID YEGANEH
In the Shadow of Islam:
The Women's Movement in Iran
Hb and Pb

BONNIE MASS
Population Target:
The Political Economy of Population Control in Latin America
Pb

NAWAL EL SAADAWI
The Hidden Face of Eve:
Women in the Arab World
Hb and Pb

ELSE SKJONSBERG
A Special Caste?
Tamil Women in Sri Lanka
Pb

PATRICIA JEFFREY
Frogs in a Well:
Indian Women in Purdah
Hb and Pb

JUNE NASH AND HELEN ICKEN SAFA (EDITORS)
Sex and Class in Latin America:
Women's Perspectives on Politics, Economics and the Family in the Third World
Pb